Christmas in Austria

A simple ceremony commemorates the creation of
"Silent Night, Holy Night"—Austria's most famous
musical contribution to the Christmas season.

At midnight mass on Christmas Eve, young
musicians in traditional dress proclaim the birth of
the Christ child (cover photo).

Christmas in Austria

From World Book

World Book Encyclopedia, Inc.

a Scott Fetzer company

Chicago

Staff

Editorial director
William H. Nault

Editorial

Executive editor
Robert O. Zeleny

Senior editor
Seva Johnson

Assistant editor
Gail L. Papke

Administrative assistant
Janet T. Peterson

Editorial assistant
Valerie Steward

Writer
Valjean McLenighan

Researcher
Kathleen L. Florio

Crafts editor
Renée Mandel

Food consultants
Nancy Odell
Ina Pinkney

Food editor
Theresa Kryst Fertig

Art

Executive art director
William Hammond

Art director
Joe Gound

Designer
Diane Hutchinson

Photography director
John S. Marshall

Photographs editors
Jo Anne Martinkus
Sandra Ozanick

Product production

Executive director
Peter Mollman

Manufacturing
Joseph C. LaCount

Research and development
Henry Koval

Pre-press services
J. J. Stack

Production control
Janice M. Rossing

Film separations
Alfred J. Mozdzen

Editorial services

Director
Susan C. Kilburg

Rights and permissions
Paul Rafferty

The editors wish to thank the many associations and private individuals in Austria and the United States who took part in developing this publication. We regret that there are so many, we cannot name them all. Special recognition, however, goes to the staff of the Austrian Consulate General in Chicago for their enthusiasm and invaluable assistance in all phases of the project.

Special appreciation also goes to Franz F. Cyrus, Press Counselor, and Annelise Adams of the Austrian Embassy, Washington, D.C., and to the Austrian Cultural Roundtable for their generous advice and assistance.

For their contributions to the photographing of Austrian foods, thanks go to Ernestine Marcoux and to the owners and staffs of the Austrian Gourmet & Tableware Co., Inc., The Crystal Cave, the Salzburg Shop, and the Vienna Pastry Shop.

English lyrics for "Wer klopfet an" (p. 11), from *Around the Year with the Trapp Family* by Maria Augusta Trapp. Copyright © 1955 by Pantheon Books, Inc. Reprinted by permission of the publisher.

English lyrics for "Jetzt hat sich halt aufgetan das himmlische Tor" (p. 48), from *The Christmas Book* by Francis X. Weiser. Copyright © 1952 by Francis X. Weiser. Reprinted by permission of Harcourt Brace Jovanovich, Inc.

"Stille Nacht, Heilige Nacht (Silent Night, Holy Night)" (pp. 74–75), arranged by Walter Ehret. "Es Wird Scho Glei Dumpa (The Twilight Is Falling)" (pp. 76–77) and "Still, Still, Still" (pp. 78–79), arranged by Walter Ehret and translated from the German by George K. Evans. From *The International Book of Christmas Carols*, copyright © 1963, 1980 by Walter Ehret and George K. Evans. Reproduced by permission of The Stephen Greene Press, Brattleboro, Vermont 05301.

Contents

Awaiting Christkindl

Straw angels, glass ornaments, hand-carved wooden Nativity scenes—Christmas decorations of every conceivable color and material tempt shoppers at the Christkindlmarkt, *or Christmas market.*

Christkindl, the Christ child, lies at the heart of Christmas in Austria. In other countries Father Christmas, Santa Claus, or St. Nicholas may fill the thoughts of children as the Christmas holidays approach. But in Austria, the Christkindl is the star of the season. It is he who brings the children their presents on Christmas Eve. The Christkindl also decorates the tree. His arrival is prepared for and celebrated with deep devotion.

One of the first signs that Christmas and the Christkindl are on their way is the appearance of the *Christkindlmarkt,* or Christmas market. Early in December these Christmas markets open in towns and cities all over Austria. The markets may be indoors or out, with rows of booths and stalls selling colorful ornaments and decorations, toys, gingerbread, Advent wreaths, candles, small gifts, and even Christmas trees. In most larger towns and cities, the Christkindlmarkt is set up in the main square. Row upon row of booths often fill the entire square, attracting Christmas shoppers both from within the city and from outlying districts.

To wander through a Christkindlmarkt is a feast for the senses. Christmas ornaments abound in every conceivable variety of color, shape, and texture. Straw angels smile benevolently upon hand-carved wooden shepherds and Wise Men. Strings of colored glass beads glitter next to boxes of large glass ornaments decorated with silver and gold sparkles. Star-shaped wax molds dangle from cross beams, each with a picture of Christkindl in the center.

It is not unusual to find artisans at work in some of the booths. Shoppers may watch a can-

A giant Weihnachtsbaum, *its branches laden with snow, towers over shoppers at Salzburg's Christmas market.*

Market booths offer tempting sweets of all kinds, including elaborate Lebkuchen hearts inscribed with holiday greetings.

Decorations in a Christkindlmarkt are seen through the eyes of schoolchildren in this delightful painting done as a class project.

*At dusk on the last Sunday before Christmas,
Austrian families light all four candles in the Advent
wreath and sing special Advent songs.*

dlemaker apply the finishing touches to a multi-colored Christmas candle. Across the aisle an artist paints an intricate design on a hand-carved angel's wing. Children wander among the stalls, carefully eyeing the dolls, chess sets, and other toys and games on display, seeking the perfect present to request from Christkindl.

In the square, shoppers wind in and out among stacks of Christmas trees, looking for the perfect *Weihnachtsbaum.* A vendor is on hand to assist them, perhaps wearing a traditional costume of Tirolean hat, hand-knit sweater, knickers, and long woolen stockings. Once a tree is chosen, it is carefully wrapped, then loaded on top of a car or wagon or bundled into a taxi for the journey home.

It is easy to work up an appetite at a Christkindlmarkt, especially when vendors offer pretzels, sausages, and paper cones filled with

roasted chestnuts for on-the-spot snacking. Other booths sell Christmas candies, sweets, and heart-shaped gingerbread cookies with Christmas greetings inscribed in colored icing. These cookie greetings are commonly given or mailed to friends.

The approach of Christmas in Austria, however, is also a time of thoughtful preparation for celebrating the birth of Jesus. Austria is a predominantly Catholic country, and many Austrians observe Advent as a solemn season of preparation for Christmas, similar to Lent, the spiritual preparation for Easter. The Advent season marks the beginning of the ecclesiastical year. It starts on the Sunday nearest November 30, which is the feast of St. Andrew, and includes the four Sundays before Christmas. The Advent season

During Advent, little girls in Oberndorf go house to house enacting the Frauentragen *and collecting money for charity.*

Little voices delight in singing Advent songs in the remaining school days before Christkindl arrives.

reminds Christians of the coming of the Christ child.

As the first Sunday in Advent approaches, many families make or purchase an *Adventkranz,* or Advent wreath. It is most often placed on a table, or it may be suspended from the ceiling with strong red ribbon. Usually fashioned from evergreen boughs, Advent wreaths come in a variety of sizes, some as large as 3 feet (90 centimeters) in diameter. They are decorated with four candles, most often red, one for each Sunday in Advent. Sometimes a larger candle is placed in the center of the wreath, symbolic of Christ, the Light of the World.

At dusk on the first Advent Sunday, the family may gather around the wreath to light a single candle and perhaps sing Advent songs or say an Advent prayer. On the second Sunday two candles are lit; on the third, three. Then on Golden Sunday—the last Sunday before Christmas—all four candles are set aglow.

Advent calendars help to build a sense of expectation in many Austrian homes. The Advent calendar may picture a mountain village scene, a house with many windows, or perhaps a kind of Jacob's ladder, like the ladder to heaven that Jacob saw in a dream. Every morning, beginning December 1, children open one little window on the calendar or "climb" a step on the ladder. Behind each window, door, or step appears a star or an angel or some other picture appropriate to the season. On Christmas Eve, December 24, the last window is opened to reveal the Christkindl smiling up from the manger.

One seldom hears a Christmas carol in Austria before December 24. The Advent season has its own special songs. "From the Heavens the Righteous Come," "O Come, O Come, Emmanuel," "Maria Wanders Through the Thorn"—these and other lovely melodies are sung and played to prepare for Christkindl's arrival. Advent songs commonly combine themes of repentance and joyous expectation of the coming of the Christ child.

Singing and musical performances play a significant role in Advent observances, as they do in most other important occasions in this music-loving country. Schoolteachers set aside classroom time to practice Advent songs. All over Austria, both children and adults don traditional costumes to celebrate the Advent in song and dance.

The *Herbergsuchen* (literally "seeking shelter") is a well-established Austrian custom, especially popular in Salzburg and Styria. There are many local variations of the tradition, which is often practiced on behalf of charity. Children go from door to door, enacting Mary and Joseph's search for a place to stay in Bethlehem, and collect money for charity. Sometimes schools or youth groups give performances based on this theme and charge admission, donating the proceeds to a worthy cause.

When practiced at home, the custom may center around a treasured religious picture—of the Annunciation, the flight into Egypt, or Mary and Joseph's search for a room in Bethlehem. The picture is hung in the parlor and decorated with evergreens and artificial flowers. For nine evenings before Christmas Eve, the family prays and sings Advent songs in front of the picture. Then the picture is mounted on a small portable platform and carried around the house—or from house to house—by the children. Each evening they perform the scene in which Mary and Joseph stand before the closed door of the inn, asking the innkeeper for a place to stay. Then they sing "Wer klopfet an," the traditional song for the Herbergsuchen.

Wer klopfet an

Who's knocking at my door?

Two people poor and low.

What are you asking for?

That you may mercy show.
We are, O Sir, in sorry plight,
O grant us shelter here tonight.

You ask in vain.

We beg a place to rest.

It's "no" again!

You will be greatly blessed.

I told you no!
You cannot stay.
Get out of here and go your way.

Another version of this custom, known as the *Frauentragen*, takes place in Oberndorf, near Salzburg. Young girls carry the image of Mary from house to house. Bearing lanterns and lighted candles, they knock at each door and announce that

The furry coat and frightening mask of this village Krampus make tempting targets for snowball throwers on Krampus Day, December 5.

December 5, St. Nicholas Eve, is known as Krampus Day in some rural areas. Krampus is an evil spirit, or minor devil, most often clad in frightening fur. He has a long tail and a long red tongue and carries a rattling chain, birch branches, and a big black bag. On Krampus Day, children and adults go together to the village square to throw snowballs at this menacing figure and otherwise try to chase him off. One or more Krampuses lie in wait, rattling chains and threatening to carry off naughty children in the big black bags or to punish the children with birch branches. But this is all done in fun, with much teasing and poking and laughter. Krampus' purpose is simply to remind children to be good, and he is especially careful not to actually frighten the little ones. In certain districts it is not children but young girls who are whisked away and deposited in the snow—evidence of Krampus' origins as a fertility demon.

St. Nicholas, the special saint of children, is widely honored throughout Austria. He is an ancestor of Santa Claus and Father Christmas, but in Austria (as in many other countries) he appears on his saint's day, a holiday separate from Christmas.

In some parts of the country he makes his appearance on St. Nicholas Eve, December 5, accompanied by Krampus. In other districts, the pair wait until December 6, the feast day of St. Nicholas. Occasionally the saint makes a solo visit. Sometimes he is never seen at all, but the children always know when he has been there. On St. Nicholas Eve they place their shoes on the windowsill, or sometimes outside their bedroom doors. St. Nicholas traditionally rewards children who have been good all year by filling their shoes with fruits, nuts, and sweets.

The historical St. Nicholas was an early Christian martyr and Bishop of Myra in Asia Minor in the fourth century. He is said to have saved three young girls from slavery by discreetly throwing alms through their window for dowries. God rewarded the bishop's generosity by giving him permission to walk the earth on his feast day, bringing gifts to all good children.

In Austria today the saint customarily appears in flowing robe and miter—the tall, pointed headdress worn by bishops. St. Nicholas carries a shepherd's staff and a thick book, in which the Guardian Angels have been keeping track all year of the good and bad deeds of the world's children. That is why he has such an astonishing knowledge of each family he visits.

At the appointed time the whole family, often including grandparents, gathers to await the saint's arrival. In he walks, accompanied by

"The heavenly mother is looking for a place to stay." At each house, money is donated to help the needy during the Christmas season.

December 4 is the feast of St. Barbara, the patron saint of miners. Workers in the gold mines at Rauris celebrate the day with "Barbara bread," a special gingerbread roll. At night they leave out food for the *Bergmannl*, or "little people."

All over Austria, "Barbara branches" are cut from cherry or pear trees, brought into houses, and placed in water on December 4. The indoor warmth creates a sort of artificial spring, and the branches come to life. It is said that the owner of the first branch to sprout a shoot can look forward to good luck in the coming year. There is another old belief that a person whose Barbara branch blossoms on Christmas Day can expect to be married in the following year.

St. Nicholas carries a book in which each child's deeds, both good and bad, have been carefully recorded by the Guardian Angels.

*This bakery display window features pastry likenesses
of St. Nicholas and his long-tongued sidekick,
Krampus. Chocolate candy decorations take the sting
out of the birch branches, which Krampus uses to
threaten naughty children.*

Krampus, who is there to deal with the children
who deserve a scolding. Nicholas (portrayed by a
friend, relative, or neighbor) calls each young
member of the household forward. He may ask
them to give an account of themselves, or perhaps to recite their prayers. When Krampus at-
tempts to punish the naughty children, the good
St. Nicholas drives him away. After each child
promises good behavior, the bishop distributes
the treats. In addition to oranges, nuts, and
sweets, St. Nicholas sometimes rewards good
children with birch branches decorated with
candy, perhaps to remind them that Krampus is
lurking about should they falter.

December 5 traditionally is the day when many
Austrian households begin to "smell like Christmas." A special kind of cookie, known as *Specu-
latius* or *Speculaas*, is baked for St. Nicholas Day.
The dough is rolled very thin and then cut in the
shapes of St. Nicholas and Krampus. Saint-
shaped cookies are decorated with icing of differ-

ent colors and candied fruit. Krampus cookies
may have raisin eyes, an almond nose, and a red
crepe-paper tongue.

For St. Nicholas Day, bakery windows display
bread baked in the shape of Krampus. Round
sandwiches may also bear the faces of Krampus
and St. Nicholas. The windows are often decorated with birch branches—reminders of the
whip with which Krampus threatens naughty
children.

Of all his public appearances, St. Nicholas' official visit to the city of Innsbruck may be the most
spectacular. A huge tree sits in the Old Town
square before the famous Golden Roof—a late-
Gothic bay window with hundreds of gold-plated
tiles, built in 1500 as a royal box from which Emperor Maximilian I could view entertainments in
the square below. Surrounded by children
dressed as shepherds, angels, and torchbearers,
St. Nicholas delivers a message of good will to
the mayor of Innsbruck. Then he lights the
town's Christmas tree in preparation for the
Christ child's arrival.

December 13, St. Lucy Day, is celebrated mainly in Lower Austria and Burgenland. On St. Lucy Eve, witches are supposed to possess extraordinary powers. Householders protect themselves against the witches' black magic by purifying their homes with blackthorn and clouds of incense.

On St. Thomas Day, December 21, the entire house is blessed and purified with incense, especially the sleeping areas and the cowsheds. Legend says that unmarried girls can see into the future on St. Thomas Night—but not without effort. They must first climb into bed over a stool and throw their shoes toward the door, toes pointing doorward. This done, if they sleep with their heads at the foot of the bed, their dreams will reward them with visions of their future husbands. The single woman who can pick out a young rooster from among a brood of sleeping chicks on St. Thomas Day will soon acquire a husband, or see him in her dreams.

Throughout the Austrian Alps, St. Thomas Day is the day for baking *Kletzenbrot*, as well as a host of other traditional Christmas treats. Though it takes its name from the Tirolean word for dried pears, Kletzenbrot actually contains a variety of dried fruits and nuts. This wholesome bread keeps for weeks and seems to improve with age. A large loaf may be baked for the family's breakfast Christmas morning, and sometimes individual smaller loaves, one for each person in the household.

On St. Thomas Day the Christmas baking begins in earnest. From then on the house is filled with the appetizing scents of *Lebkuchen, Pfeffernüsse, Stollen,* and the many other delicacies for which the Austrians are justly famous.

Amid the many Advent activities and adult preparations, the children are busily making some plans of their own. Christkindl is much in their thoughts, for it is Christkindl who will bring the new dolls and trains, games, bicycles, or other delights they will receive on Christmas Eve.

The Christkindl Church, near Steyr, is built around the tree where Ferdinand Sertl long ago placed a little wax statue of the infant Jesus and was miraculously cured.

Traditionally, Austrian youngsters write to Christkindl early in Advent to tell him of their hearts' desires. The Christmas wish list is carefully placed in a window or on a windowsill where the Christ child or one of his angel helpers will be sure to see it. By the following morning the letter is invariably gone.

A modern variant of this old custom has grown up in the past few decades, centered in the town of Christkindl. For a hamlet of fewer than a hundred houses, Christkindl has a fascinating history. It goes back to the late 1600's, when Ferdinand Sertl, variously described as an organist, watchman, and "poor young woodcutter," suffered from epilepsy and other diseases.

Kletzenbrot
(Christmas fruit bread)

3 cups flour
⅔ cup brown sugar
3 tsp. baking powder
2 tsp. baking soda
¼ tsp. salt

2 cups buttermilk
1 cup chopped nuts
1 cup chopped prunes
1 cup diced dates or figs
1 cup raisins

1. Blend all dry ingredients together. Add buttermilk slowly, stirring to make a smooth dough.

2. Stir in nuts and fruits.

3. Grease and flour a 10-inch tube pan. Spoon batter into pan.

4. Bake at 350° for 45 minutes.

Yield: 1 loaf

In 1695 nuns from a convent near Steyr took pity on Sertl and gave him a small wax statue of the infant Jesus. Sertl took the statue into the woods above Steyr, carved a niche in a big pine tree, and placed his treasure in the niche.

Every week Sertl climbed the steep, narrow path to the top of the hill to pray at his shrine for relief from his sickness. His perseverance was rewarded. Sertl's illnesses gradually became less severe and finally disappeared altogether.

The nuns who donated the statue for Sertl's shrine were duly impressed and lost little time in spreading word of the miraculous cure. Soon pilgrims began to visit the shrine to "the Christ child under the heavens."

As early as 1697, an enclosure was built around the tree, and in 1703 the Bishop of Passau ordered a church raised on the site. The cornerstone was laid on May 31, 1708, and construction was completed under the supervision of architect Jacob Prandtauer. The ornate design, by Carlo Antonio Carlone, incorporates the living tree as the centerpiece of the altar. The niche and statue can still be seen today.

Local residents began to build their homes in the glade around the church, and soon a hamlet developed. What better name for the new community than Christkindl—or Christkindl Unterhimmel ("Christ child under the heavens"), as it is sometimes called.

More than two centuries passed relatively uneventfully. But in 1950 the Austrian Postal Administration set up its first official Christmas post office in temporary headquarters in the taproom of the village inn, "At the Sign of the Heavenly View."

That first season, a lone employee handled some 42,000 pieces of Christmas mail. Today the Christkindl post office—*Postamt Christkindl*—has enlarged its staff to 18 clerks. They handle more than a million letters, packages, and requests each year between late November and January 6.

Children address their letters to Christkindl in care of the Christkindl post office. If a parent encloses a self-addressed reply envelope, the child receives a special Christmas greeting in response. The greeting bears the Christkindl postmark—a stamp showing the Holy Family under the Christmas star.

Letters and parcels from all over Austria are routed through the Christkindl post office to receive the special stamp. Postamt Christkindl also gets letters from children throughout the world.

Quite a few of the parcels in the Austrian mails at Christmastime emit the tantalizing aromas of cookies, pastries, and other baked goods in transit. *Stollen*, a Christmas coffee cake, is a special favorite. In some families, the godmother traditionally gives or sends her godchild a Christmas Stollen as a gift. This dry, cakelike bread is often gift-wrapped in clear cellophane and tied with a bow of red ribbon. Stollen is usually stored for at least three days before it is eaten, and it keeps well for several weeks. No Austrian Christmas would be complete without it.

As the Advent season draws to a close, greetings are exchanged, cookies baked, and other preparations for Christkindl's arrival proceed with mounting excitement. The tempting odors of Lebkuchen, Stollen, Pfeffernüsse, and other Christmas delicacies waft through city streets and village lanes. Spirits rise like the refrain of one of the most beautiful of all the Advent songs: "Freue dich, Christkind kommt bald!" "Rejoice, for the Christ child is coming soon!"

Children laugh on their way home from the Christkindl post office, which annually processes more than a million pieces of Christmas mail from all over the world.

A child places a thoughtfully written wish list in the window for Christkindl or an angel helper to find.

Stacks of fragrant Christmas Stollen, wrapped in cellophane and ribbons, grace this display window in the Cafe Aida.

Stollen
(Christmas bread)

2 packages dry yeast
¼ cup very warm water (110°)
¾ cup milk at room temperature or
    slightly warmed
½ cup sugar
½ tsp. salt
½ cup unsalted butter, softened
2 large eggs plus 1 additional egg
    yolk, lightly beaten together
4¾ cups all-purpose flour
1 cup raisins or currants (or a 1-cup
    mixture of both)
½ cup diced citron
½ cup diced candied orange peel
    or other candied fruit
¾ cup chopped blanched almonds
2 tsp. cinnamon
½ cup confectioners' sugar for
    dusting

1. Mix yeast with the water and stir to dissolve. Add the milk, salt, sugar, butter, and the 2 whole eggs plus the yolk from the third egg. Blend well.

2. Dust the raisins (or currants), citron, and candied orange peel (or candied fruit) with a little of the flour, and then add the almonds. Mix in the cinnamon, and set fruit and nut mixture aside.

3. Add half the flour to the yeast mixture and stir until smooth. Cover and let rise in a warm place until doubled in bulk—about 1 hour.

4. Add the remaining flour and knead until smooth and elastic— about 5 minutes. Knead in the fruit and nut mixture.

5. Place the dough in an oiled bowl, turning the dough so it is completely coated. Cover and let rise for about 30 minutes.

6. Divide the dough into 2 equal portions. Press 1 portion of the dough into a large flat circle. Fold 1 side of the circle of dough over so that the top half is 1 inch from the edge of the bottom half, forming a split loaf shape. Repeat this step with the remaining portion of dough.

7. Place each loaf on a greased baking sheet, cover with plastic wrap, and let rise again until doubled in size—about 30 minutes.

8. Bake at 375° for 40 minutes until golden brown. Cool on wire rack. Sprinkle top generously with confectioners' sugar before serving.

Yield: 2 loaves

An Austrian Family Christmas

Spanish Wind cookies hang from the branches of this lovely tree, while a bird, stars, and a Christkindl dressed in swaddling clothes float nearby.

Christmas in Austria, more than any other time of year, is a holiday celebrated by and for families. Outside it is almost always cold, with snow covering the ground. But inside, Austrian homes radiate the special warmth of the season. Family members who do not see one another at other times of the year make a special effort to get together sometime over the Christmas holidays. *Weihnachtszeit*—Christmastime—is filled with happy moments for youngsters and adults alike.

During the weeks before Christmas, Austrian streets and shopwindows, from the larger cities to the tiniest hamlets, are festooned with evergreens and twinkling colored lights. Toyshops, department stores, bakeries, and other establishments often set up special Christmas displays.

Most Austrian communities erect a big public Weihnachtsbaum in the main square or some other central location and decorate it with strings of electric lights and fancy ornaments. Small villages often compete to see who has the best tree. Evergreens in public parks may be hung with birdseed or breadcrumb decorations, much to the delight of the feathered members of the community. Christmas trees can also be found in hotels and restaurants, coffee houses and theater lobbies, the waiting rooms of railway stations—in short, anywhere and everywhere.

The lovely custom of lighting and decorating small trees at Christmastime seems to have originated in Germany. One legend traces it to St. Boniface, who in the 700's left England to take on the task of converting the Germans to Christianity. Yet another tradition attributes the Weihnachtsbaum to Martin Luther. He is said to have used a

The typical Austrian family Christmas tree is still lit by the warm glow of candlelight on Christmas Eve.

candlelit tree to remind his flock of the starry heavens on Christmas Eve.

The first Christmas tree of which we have historical evidence is described in a 1605 diary kept by an anonymous visitor to Strasbourg. The author writes of fir trees set up in parlors and decorated with apples, flat wafers, candies, sugar, and paper roses in a variety of shades. The rose was frequently employed in early Christian art as a symbol of the Virgin Mary. The flat wafers are clearly reminiscent of communion wafers, which symbolize the body of Christ. In Austria, a tree hung with such wafers, or with cookies decorated with religious designs, came to be known as a *Christbaum*. The practice of erecting a Christbaum to honor the Christ child's birthday was spreading in Austria during the early 1600's.

The Christbaum also appeared in other forms in the 1600's and 1700's. In some parts of Austria, holiday-makers cut the tips from large evergreens and hung them upside down in living room or parlor corners, often decorated with apples, candied nuts, and red paper strips. The corner was referred to as "the Lord God's corner." Still another custom was to hang the evergreen tips in windows or from ceiling rafters, right side up. The butt was sharpened to a point, from which an apple was suspended.

For several generations, the Christbaum seems to have existed side by side with a candlelit, artificial tree called a *Lichtstock*. Evergreen branches were wrapped around open, pyramid-shaped wooden frames and then decorated with candles and pastry. Eventually the candles were transferred to the Christbaum, and the Lichtstock fell by the wayside.

Though the Christmas tree was fully ornamented and widely accepted throughout Austria by the 1700's, the custom was not adopted by Austrian royalty until the early part of the 1800's. Around 1815 a German princess of Nassau Weilburg paid a winter call on the royal house of Hapsburg. She introduced the Weihnachtsbaum to Emperor Francis I, and from then on the Austrian royal family included a tree in its Christmas celebrations.

Today the Weihnachtsbaum is at the heart of the Austrian family Christmas. In fact, it plays a central role throughout the holiday season.

Many children busy themselves near the end of Advent making ornaments for the family Christmas tree—from colored paper, foil, ribbons, or bits and pieces of any other material that comes to hand. They may wrap nuts and candy with foil or tissue paper and attach colored thread so that the Christ child can hang the ornaments easily when he and the angel helpers decorate the Christmas tree. Other materials are fashioned into suns, moons, shooting stars, angels, tiny Christmas trees, trumpets, and more—the only limits are set by the youngsters' imaginations.

In Austria, Christmas is a time for children. School activities reflect the fact that Christmas is the most important holiday on the calendar. During the last few days before Christmas, school plays that were written and rehearsed earlier in December are finally performed for parents and other relatives and friends. Mothers and fathers busy with their own holiday preparations may interrupt their work to mend a broken angel's wing or to answer a frantic last-minute plea for help in constructing a cardboard manger.

Most families will make at least one Christmas shopping trip together, perhaps dropping hints about desirable Christmas presents as they gaze in wonder at the wealth of delights displayed in the local Christkindlmarkt and in store windows. Then, of course, the gifts are purchased and wrapped in secret and hidden from the rest of the family until Christmas Eve.

The period just before Christmas Eve is a time of last-minute baking. Homemade gingerbread houses are baked, constructed, and decorated with loving care. *Spanische Windbäckerei*, or Spanish Wind cookies, are another traditional favorite. These meringue confections, light as the wind, are baked in the shape of little Christmas wreaths and are often used as ornaments for the Weihnachtsbaum.

Spanische Windbäckerei
(Spanish Wind meringue cookies)

4 egg whites (½ cup)
¼ tsp. cream of tartar
¾ cup sugar

1. Preheat oven to 350°. Line large cookie sheet with aluminum foil.

2. Beat egg whites until foamy. Add cream of tartar and continue beating until stiff. Gradually add sugar—1 Tbsp. at a time—beating after each addition. Beat at high speed 3 minutes after last addition.

3. Pipe batter into the form of small wreaths on cookie sheet, using pastry bag fitted with open star tube. Sprinkle with decorating crystals.

4. Place in preheated oven and immediately turn off heat. Leave in oven overnight. Do *not* open oven door during this time.

These cookies are beautiful tied with ribbons to the Christmas tree.

Yield: about 3–5 dozen cookies, depending on size

Star-crowned angels and furry-headed farm animals visit the Holy Family in this schoolroom Nativity play performed for admiring parents.

The whole family may join in selecting the Christmas tree, which Christkindl and the angels will decorate—with a little help from Mother and Father.

In some families, the parents go in secret to purchase the Christmas tree, which is kept out of the children's sight until Christmas Eve. Other families go together to the Christmas tree lot, carefully scrutinizing each pine and balsam before making a final selection.

Austrian children do not see the decorated family tree until Christmas Eve. It is secreted behind the closed doors of the "Christmas room"—at other times of the year known as the living room or parlor. For several days before the big event, the Christmas room is off-limits to children. The Christ child and his angels are decorating the family tree, with occasional assistance from Mother, Father, or other adults in the family. Children need not apply.

Christmas Eve is the traditional time to exchange gifts with friends and family. Shops close by 6 P.M. The curtains drop in movie houses,

23

During a last-minute shopping trip, a Viennese family considers what Christkindl might bring on Christmas Eve.

theaters, and concert halls. Restaurants and nightclubs grow silent and dark. Traffic seems to disappear.

Most Austrian homes enter the final stages of preparation for Christkindl's arrival. For the children the excitement is almost unbearable. Adults tiptoe about and communicate in whispers. Mother and Father may spend much of the day behind the closed doors of the Christmas room. Every so often they are interrupted by a quiet knock at the door. They open it to the sound of receding footsteps and look down to find a stack of Christmas presents, each one with a name tag. Parents are not the only ones with Christmas Eve surprises!

Grandparents, uncles, aunts, and cousins often arrive in the early evening. Candles are placed in the windows as a symbolic greeting to absent friends and relatives, and in memory of those who have passed away.

Finally, the children hear the sound they have all been awaiting—the tinkling bell that summons them to the Christmas room. There, for the first time that season, they witness Christkindl's handiwork.

Each year's Weihnachtsbaum seems the most magical ever. Dozens and dozens of cookies are tied to the branches with colored thread or ribbon; small apples and tangerines may dangle from the lower limbs. Decorations often include angels, birds, and other creatures made of wood and straw, or wax stars bearing pictures of the infant Jesus. Christkindl may also appear wrapped in swaddling clothes or even enjoying himself on a sled. Then there are the children's homemade ornaments and other handcrafted decorations—some, perhaps, which have been treasured for generations. Silver and gold garlands crisscross the tree like threads of a dew-decked spider's web. Tinsel shimmers gently from every branch.

Best of all, the whole magical creation glows softly in the light of scores of wax candles and sparklers. While electric lights are commonly used to decorate community Christmas trees, most Austrian families would never dream of lighting their own trees with anything other than the traditional Christmas candles. Next to the tree

Creamy frosting holds cookie shingles in place on the roof of this homemade gingerbread house. The whole family may join in to add the brightly colored candies and frostings that will complete the decoration.

they place a camouflaged bucket of water and a long-handled mop to be used in case of emergency. Generally, however, everyone keeps such a close watch on the tree that emergencies do not arise.

Almost every family in Austria also has a *Krippe* or manger scene, with miniature figures of the newborn Christ child and his parents. Often the figures are dressed in traditional Austrian costumes. A Krippe may have only a few figures— perhaps the Holy Family, a shepherd or two, and a couple of animals. But other families display very elaborate scenes, with dozens of hand-carved shepherds, animals, and other figures. Some families keep adding new characters and scenery each year, especially if an uncle, grandfather, or other family member is a talented woodcarver. Often these mangers are hundreds of years old, treasured heirlooms handed down from one generation to the next.

Lebkuchen, *perhaps the most popular Austrian Christmas cookies, are patiently decorated with icing, cherries, and almonds.*

There's nothing quite like the magical moment when the little ones see the decorated tree for the first time.

The Nativity scene placed under the tree bears each family's personal touches. Here, the children have added evergreen twigs, stones, grass, and a bed of snowy cotton.

26

The Krippe is usually placed under the Christmas tree, next to the presents. It may be set up before Christmas Eve, especially if it is an elaborate Krippe. But Christkindl is not placed in the manger until Christmas Eve.

After the birthday of Baby Jesus has been so recognized, and everyone has had a chance to admire the tree and Nativity scene, the family members lift their voices in song. "Silent Night, Holy Night," the beautiful carol composed in 1818 in the Austrian village of Oberndorf, is still a time-honored favorite. In other countries, this carol may be played on the radio and television, in stores, and in restaurants during the weeks before Christmas. But in Austria "Silent Night" is heard for the first time on Christmas Eve, and the effect is spellbinding.

Other carols, of folk or classical origin, are also sung with gusto in the family home on Christmas Eve. "The Twilight Is Falling," "Still, Still, Still," "Above, on the Mountain," and "A Baby in the Cradle" may be followed by Christmas poems and readings that have been painstakingly memorized by the family's younger members. And someone may relate the most important story of all—the story of the Nativity itself.

The adults and children exchange the traditional Christmas greeting: *Fröhliche Weihnachten!* Merry Christmas! In some families, members wish one another a blessed Christmas—*Gesegnete Weihnachten.*

Finally the children are free to turn their attention to the gifts under the tree. Everyone joins in the exchange of presents, the *Bescherung.* Sweaters are tried on for size, games are unwrapped, and gleaming new toys are admired by one and all. For the next hour or so, the Christmas room is filled with happy exclamations.

With all this excitement, of course, the whole family has worked up a hearty appetite. The typical Christmas Eve dinner consists of a main course of carp, since the day is traditionally a fast day. The fish is usually accompanied by potato salad, a fish soup, and a variety of tortes, cookies, or other sweets for dessert. The carp may be baked or broiled or dipped in flour, eggs, and breadcrumbs and fried in deep fat until golden brown.

A traditional and very popular method is to boil the carp *au bleu* in a court bouillon with vinegar. When boiled in the vinegar, the fish actually does turn blue. More adventurous cooks may prepare Polish-style carp in aspic or serve the fish cold with a Hungarian paprika sauce. Sometimes the fish is baked in black sauce, especially in families partial to Czech-style cooking.

As midnight approaches, it is time to get ready for mass. In many churches—such as St. Stephen's in Vienna, where thousands attend midnight mass on Christmas Eve—trumpeters climb to the church towers and trumpet forth Christmas music to call the faithful to worship. The *Turmblasen*—brass instruments playing chorale music from the city tower or steeple of the main church—is a traditional feature of Christmas Eve.

Churches lacking trumpeters often send their best carolers to the church towers to guide parishioners on their way to mass. As likely as not, rural families will hold torches in their hands as they wend their way down from the mountains to attend services in the valley. These long, torchlight processions make Christmas Eve a dramatic and memorable occasion.

Nativity plays and mystery pageants are widely popular at Christmastime. In the past, these *Christi-Geburtsspiele* were performed as part of the

Pfeffernüsse
(peppernut cookies)

The secret of good "peppernuts" is to ripen the dough 2–3 days before baking and to store the cookies 1–2 weeks before eating.

3 cups all-purpose flour
1 tsp. cinnamon
⅛ tsp. cloves
¼ tsp. white pepper
3 eggs
1 cup sugar
⅓ cup very finely chopped blanched almonds
⅓ cup very finely chopped candied orange peel and citron

1. Mix flour and spices and set aside.

2. Beat eggs until foamy and slowly add sugar. Continue beating until thick and lemon-colored. Slowly mix in flour, then almonds, then orange peel and citron.

3. Wrap dough in foil and refrigerate for 2–3 days.

4. When ready to bake, roll dough into 1-inch balls. Space balls 2 inches apart on greased baking sheet.

5. Bake at 350° for 15–20 minutes. Cool on wire rack. Store in a covered container for 1–2 weeks.

6. Dredge cookies in confectioners' sugar before serving.

Yield: about 3 dozen cookies

midnight mass, and in some rural churches this tradition is still alive. Children and adults act out the numerous stories surrounding the birth of Christ. The Annunciation and the Nativity are two common themes. The various shepherds who came to the manger to worship the newborn Christ child are much beloved in Austria, as are the Three Wise Men. Another popular story is that of the Holy Family's flight into Egypt to escape persecution by Herod's soldiers. These folk dramas are often enacted in local dialect by performers wearing traditional Austrian costumes.

As the service comes to a close, the priest blesses his parishioners and sends them out into the small hours of Christmas morning. Crowds of sleepy adults and youngsters wend their way home through the Christmas snows. Those who are awake enough may snack on leftover pastries, or perhaps enjoy a plate of sausages before retiring. But others dive straight under their comforters, exhausted from the day's excitement.

Christmas Day is one of quiet celebration and happy reunions with family and friends. Some families will attend mass again on Christmas Day before gathering the family together for the holiday dinner.

As is true of most important occasions in Austria, the Christmas holiday is fueled by a variety of tempting specialties to eat and drink. At breakfast the family most likely will enjoy the Kletzenbrot baked on St. Thomas Day, December 21, or perhaps a Stollen. Throughout Christmas Day, friends and relatives who come to visit may be offered a glass of wine or a fragrant—and potent—*Weihnachtspunsch*.

Christmas dinner typically begins with a soup course. This is usually a rich beef broth with tiny dumplings or bits of thin pancakes floating in it. A traditional entree is roast goose stuffed with apples or prunes or chestnuts. Other popular alternatives are roast pork, ham, and *Wiener Schnitzel*—the lightly breaded veal cutlet, originated in Austria and savored around the world. Roasted potatoes and red cabbage or sauerkraut often accompany the main course, with other side dishes of roasted apples, stewed prunes or apricots, and a salad of cabbage or other greens.

For those who can still manage to eat dessert, an array of temptations is offered. A nut, apple, or poppy seed strudel is almost always included. There might also be a Christmas Stollen or cake and assorted other pastries and cookies. The dinner is washed down with generous glasses of wine and is usually followed by coffee. After dinner, the Christmas tree is lit again, and everyone joins in singing carols.

Weihnachtspunsch
(Christmas punch)

1 stick cinnamon
½ tsp. whole cloves
grated rind of 1 lemon
grated rind of 1 orange
1 lb. sugar
2 cups water

1. Bring the spices and water to a boil. Strain and put flavored liquid into a large pot.
2. Add:
1 pineapple, sliced
juice of 4 small lemons
juice of 4 medium oranges
1 bottle of red wine
1 bottle of claret

3. Cover and heat. Remove punch from the heat before it boils.
4. Add:
1 bottle champagne
5. Serve.

The Christmas Eve midnight mass at St. Stephen's Cathedral in Vienna draws upwards of 9000 persons to celebrate the birth of the Christ child.

On Christmas Day and St. Stephen's Day, families and friends traditionally share elaborate dinners, seasoned with good holiday spirit.

After Christmas dinner, these Austrian boys find time to play with their new games.

By the evening of Christmas Day, most of Austria's theaters, movie houses, concert halls, and nightclubs have reopened after their Christmas Eve silence. Many families finish Christmas Day by attending a performance together. Those with the time and means might leave for a winter ski vacation or for a holiday visit with relatives in another city or town.

December 26, St. Stephen's Day, is a legal holiday from work and school, a day set aside for visiting. In the streets and squares one is likely to see crowds of people milling about, many sporting brand-new scarves or sweaters. Children will be carrying their favorite new toys.

St. Stephen, the first Christian martyr, is also the patron saint of horses. There are no less than sixteen pageants celebrated in the saint's honor in various parts of Austria, as well as numerous horse shows and races. In the Salzburg area, people still bake bread in the shape of horseshoes to celebrate the day.

The province of Carinthia alone has eight St. Stephen's pageants. In Lind, church altars are draped with red cloth for the feast day mass. The cloth is then cut into pieces, which are distributed after church as good luck charms for horses.

In medieval times, the Twelve Nights after Christmas were a period of rest for domestic animals. The horse, an exceptionally useful four-legged creature, was accorded a feast day of its own.

Up until World War II, Austrian farmers commonly decorated their horses on St. Stephen's Day, weaving ribbons through the animals' manes and tails. After a solemn high mass, the priest would bless the animals with holy water and sprinkler. He also blessed the hay and oats used to feed them. The practice still exists in some areas, but it is no longer typical.

In the quiet of Christmas Night, the lovely city of Salzburg glistens under a fresh dusting of snow.

Christmas Eve, Christmas Day, St. Stephen's Day: these three feast days combine to form the highest holiday in Austria. Christmas is a time for strengthening family ties, renewing faith, and exchanging tokens of love and appreciation with relatives and friends. It is a holiday with a distinctly religious cast, for, after all, it celebrates the birth of Jesus. But in Austria the winter revels do not cease on St. Stephen's Night. In fact, December 26 marks the opening of festivities with a decidedly more secular flavor—the magical, mysterious Twelve Nights after Christmas.

The Twelve Nights and Sylvester

Trumpeters stationed in city halls and church steeples herald the arrival of the New Year in cities and towns all over Austria. These red-robed musicians are in Innsbruck.

St. Stephen's Day, December 26, starts the period known as the Twelve Nights, whose mysterious activities are a blend of secular and religious traditions. Called the *Rauhnächte* (Raw Nights), the period ends on the feast of the Epiphany, January 6, which commemorates the arrival at the stable in Bethlehem of the Three Wise Men from the East. Austria celebrates the New Year with noise and gaiety—much like the rest of the world, but with a distinctly musical twist, as one would expect of a nation with such a brilliant artistic heritage. Vienna, it has been said, plunges into each new year "with music on her lips and in her heart."

The Twelve Nights begin as midnight approaches on Christmas Day, St. Stephen's Eve. According to legend, the animals in their stables begin to look around, anxiously checking out doors and windows to make sure that no one is watching. Once convinced that they are quite alone, the animals put their heads together and tell each other about their experiences during the past year. Then they talk of what the coming year will bring. The gift of speech on Holy Night is God's reward to the animals for the burdens they must bear during the rest of the year. In many legends, water turns to wine during Holy Night, and treasures can be discovered.

During the dark, stormy Twelve Nights, the one-eyed god Woden is said to gallop through the sky on his eight-legged horse, Sleipnir, leading the Wild Host. One superstition holds that the only way to avoid being kidnapped is to throw oneself into the left track of the road. Woden and his horse are the legendary ancestors

The Vienna Philharmonic annually brings in the New Year with polkas and waltzes by Strauss.

Fireworks over Salzburg are a sure sign that
Sylvesterabend, *or New Year's Eve, has ended and*
New Year's Day has begun.

of the *Goldenes Roessel* (the Golden Horse), which
in some parts of Austria brought gifts to the children before St. Nicholas and Christkindl took
over. The Golden Horse generally tried to avoid
being seen. But a person who observed a strict
fast until noon could sometimes catch a glimpse
of the magnificent creature galloping over a
rooftop.

In pagan times the winter solstice marked the
beginning of the year. But in 1691, Pope Innocent
XII formally declared January 1 to be New Year's
Day. In Austria, New Year's Eve is called *Sylvesterabend* (the Eve of St. Sylvester). The last day of
the year is dedicated to the pope who baptized
Constantine the Great, thereby initiating an en-
tirely new era as well as a new year.

As with the other Twelve Nights, New Year's

celebrations combine pagan and religious elements. In the old days, Austrian taverns and inns
were decorated with greens. A large wreath was
hung from the ceiling in the largest room, and a
strange character known as Sylvester lurked in a
dark corner. Ancient and ugly, Sylvester wore a
flaxen beard and a mistletoe wreath on his head.
Anyone who passed beneath the evergreen
wreath—young or old, man or woman—was
likely to receive a rough hug and kiss from the
gnarled old character. But when midnight came
around, Sylvester was banished, like the old
year.

New Year's Eve is celebrated with noise and
merrymaking. Confetti, streamers, and champagne are all part of family celebrations. At the
bottom of all the commotion is a belief that evil
spirits should be chased away along with the old
year. *Böller*, or miniature mortars, are fired,

This Austrian bakery displays an impressive selection of good luck gifts for the New Year, including marzipan mushrooms and sweet candy pigs. Carnival jelly doughnuts also tempt window shoppers.

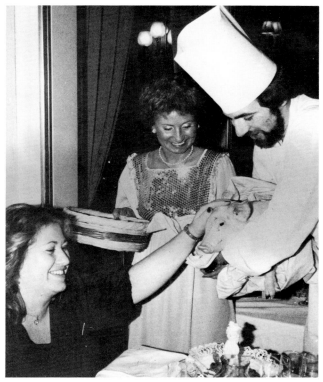

Austrians know that touching a pig on New Year's Eve brings good fortune. This chef is creating his own luck—and his friend with the basket is collecting the tips. Diners receive a candy pig as a souvenir.

church bells ring, and trumpets sound. In some of the larger cities, revellers are treated to midnight fireworks displays.

Austrians believe that a new year should have a positive beginning. Pork is a favorite food for New Year's celebrations. The traditional entree is suckling pig, roasted to perfection. Perhaps this tradition goes back to the ancient custom of sacrificing a wild boar in honor of the new year. It is also said that the pig brings good luck because it moves forward as it furrows along the ground with its snout. On the other hand, many Austrians would refuse to eat a crayfish or lobster on New Year's Eve because these creatures move backward.

A few of Vienna's finest restaurants offer an amusing variation of the good-luck pig tradition. On New Year's Eve, chefs or waiters bring a live pig into their elegant dining rooms, and the diners may touch the pig for good luck.

New Year's Eve in Vienna offers a variety of other ways to mark the occasion. Attending midnight mass at St. Stephen's is one of Vienna's traditions. Those who wish to bring in the year with music may attend the opera or the symphony. The popular Strauss operetta *Die Fledermaus* is presented every New Year's Eve and New Year's Day at the Vienna State Opera. On the afternoon of December 31, the Vienna Philharmonic presents an all-Strauss concert of waltzes and polkas. A repeat performance of this concert on New Year's Day is televised throughout Europe and is broadcast in many countries around the world.

In the countryside, people either go to a restaurant or enjoy New Year's Eve dinner at home. All over Austria, midnight is signalled by the blowing of trumpets from church towers, a custom also observed on Christmas Eve. People customarily exchange kisses, expressing their feelings of good will. Everyone offers wishes of good health, success, and, in the countryside, an abundant harvest.

New Year's Eve begins the annual Carnival season, known as *Fasching*, which lasts until the beginning of Lent. All over Austria, gala balls and parties mark the weeks of Fasching, launched by the Emperor's Ball in Vienna on New Year's Eve. The highlight of the Vienna Fasching season is the Opera Ball, held later in February. A favorite delicacy for the Carnival season is *Faschingskrapfen,* or Carnival jelly donuts. Austrians start enjoying

these delightful donuts on New Year's Eve as Fasching gets underway.

Good luck symbols called *Glücksbringer* are customarily exchanged on New Year's Eve and Day. Chocolate and marzipan are shaped into pigs, gold coins, chimney sweeps, four-leaf clovers, and even horseshoes. In the villages, New Year's morning is usually celebrated by attending mass. Children go from house to house singing New Year's songs and offering good wishes. In some places a choir or band serenades door-to-door.

There's a long-standing belief that everything one does on January 1 indicates how the rest of the year will go. If one is late that day, one is likely to be late for many of the days to come. Someone who sees a chimney sweep first thing on the morning of January 1 is sure to have an excellent year. But it's a very bad omen if the first person one encounters is an old woman.

Many Austrian New Year's traditions have to do with predicting the future. One sure way of finding out what the coming year will bring is by "pouring lead." Everyone gathers round the fireplace or stove, where lead buttons or pieces of old lead pipe are melted in an iron ladle. The ladle is held over an open fire or candle, and the melted lead is then poured into a bucket of cold water. The lead hardens into all kinds of strange shapes, called *Bleigiessen.*

Every group has at least one soothsayer—someone with a knack for interpreting the "lead language." A lump in the shape of a boat, train, or car is a sure sign that someone is about to

Faschingskrapfen
(Carnival jelly doughnuts)

¼ cup granulated sugar
1 cup warm milk (110°)
2 packages dry yeast
4 cups all-purpose flour
½ tsp. salt
2 to 3 Tbsp. oil
2 egg yolks
½ cup jam
oil for deep frying
confectioners' sugar for dusting

1. Stir 1 tsp. of the granulated sugar into the warm milk and sprinkle yeast over milk. Let stand for 5 minutes or until the surface is frothy.

2. Blend flour, remaining granulated sugar, and salt into a large bowl and set aside.

3. In a medium bowl, blend the 2–3 Tbsp. oil and egg yolks. Add the yeast mixture.

4. Pour egg and yeast mixture into flour mixture and beat until a stiff dough is formed. Cover and let rise for 20 minutes in a warm place.

5. On a floured surface, roll out the dough to a ½-inch thickness. Cut out 3-inch rounds.

6. Place a teaspoon of jam in the center of a round, and carefully place another round on top. Press edges firmly together. Using a 2½-inch round cookie cutter, press down on dough to seal edges. Remove scraps. Reroll scraps and cut additional rounds.

7. Cover with a towel and let rise for about 30 minutes until rather plump.

8. Heat the oil to 360° in a deep pot with a lid. Place doughnuts, smooth topside down, into the hot oil. Cover and cook 2–3 minutes until golden brown. Turn them over and fry, uncovered, until golden brown. Drain on paper towels and dust with confectioners' sugar.

Note: Be sure to use enough oil so that the doughnuts can "swim" in the oil. Then you will get the pale band around the middle that is distinctive of Faschingskrapfen.

Faschingskrapfen are best when eaten immediately, when they are warm and very fresh.

Yield: about 1 dozen doughnuts

Viennese society still dances its traditional waltz at
the Opera Ball, the highlight of the Fasching *season.*

On the last of the Twelve Nights, specially blessed chalk is used to mark the initials of the Three Kings and the number of the year over each door.

A farmer burns incense in a pan of charcoal to purify his barn and animals. His daughter sprinkles holy water to bless them on the last of the Twelve Nights.

leave on a journey. The Bleigiessen often show that a letter full of surprises is in the mail, or, for a lucky few, that money is on the way. Those who are unmarried almost always learn that a new or old flame is in their new year's picture.

In certain parts of the country, unmarried girls throw their slippers behind them. From the way the slippers fall, the young women can learn whether they will step to the altar that year.

The clamor of New Year's celebrations may come to an end, but the mysterious Twelve Nights are still running their course. In earlier times, the nights between Christmas and Epiphany were called "Smoke Nights," because the people went through their houses and barns burning incense and blessing their homesteads. Today this practice persists on only one night— the last and most "dangerous" of the Twelve Nights, January 6. The head of the household or the oldest servant moves through the farm buildings with a pan or shovel full of charcoal, on which incense is burned to smoke out evil spirits. A young member of the family assists in the annual rite by sprinkling holy water liberally over house, grounds, and barns. After the whole

homestead has been blessed, the head of the household marks the transoms of all the doors in chalk, writing the initials thought to be those of the Three Wise Men—K(aspar) + M(elchior) + B(althasar)—and the number of the year. These three letters have supplanted the pagan *Drudenfuss* (pentagram) that once prevented evil spirits from entering peasant homes.

In rural Austria, the Twelve Nights are also observed with long processions of elaborately masked and costumed characters, sometimes blowing horns or cracking whips. These have evolved from ancient purification rites, intended to drive away ghosts and evil spirits. In certain areas, they also derive from spring rituals that are hundreds of years older than the Christian feasts they now observe. These processions take different forms in different regions of Austria, but all are colorful and exciting.

In the Pongau area of Land Salzburg, as in other Alpine regions, a tradition called the *Perchtenlauf* is observed. The Perchtenlauf, held in Gasteinertal every four years, is a centuries-old tradition. According to an ancient story, Frau Perchta was a half-human and half-divine creature with supernatural powers. She was ex-

Elaborate headdresses are characteristic of the processions in rural Austria that take place during the Twelve Nights and the Fasching *season.*

tremely unpredictable, for her nature was both very good and very evil. Sometimes she traveled through the land as a gracious character, bestowing blessings and fertility, a symbol of the good and beautiful. At other times, ugly and gloomy, with tousled hair and a long, pointed nose, she blustered about, bringing misfortune and ruin to all.

In the Perchtenlauf, the various participants, called *Perchten,* are costumed to represent the nature and qualities of Frau Perchta. Because she is both good and evil, some of the characters are "good" Perchten and others are "bad" Perchten.

The Perchten costumes used in Gasteinertal have been handed down from one generation to the next. All the participants, even those dressed as women, are men and boys from local farms. The Perchtenlauf costumes are quite elaborate. The headdresses may be several meters (several yards) high and weigh up to 50 kilograms (110 pounds). Good Perchten caps are decorated with necklaces, watch chains, gold coins, bright flowers, and Christmas decorations. To the bad group belong the table Perchten, who wear boards on their heads hung with dead cats, mice, snakes,

old brooms, and other ugly and terrifying objects. Witches, goblins, and devils wear brightly colored carved-wood masks. Hunter Perchten may wear stag antlers, stuffed birds, or stuffed heads of fox, marten, polecat, or bison. The parade includes many other figures, such as an itinerant tinker, a knife grinder, an oil carrier, a big-beaked figure, a basket girl, and King Herod. Each character wears a wide leather belt around his waist, to which he ties heavy rolls of bells.

On the eve of the Epiphany, when Frau Perchta traditionally was at her wildest, the parade participants gather at a place known only to them. After an address by the captain, the parade gets underway, led by a small band of musicians. At the rear, an animal trainer with a bear on a chain keeps crowds from breaking into the parade.

Farmers and townspeople gladly receive the good Perchten, since they bring best wishes for happiness and fertility. After the Perchten do a short dance, the homeowners offer them refreshments. Meanwhile the bad Perchten and witches

39

In the Glöcklerlauf, *the bellringers' white costumes symbolize the purity of spring. Bells and noisemakers help to drive away the cold winter.*

are up on the roof, throwing snowballs, dumping snow down the chimney, and otherwise creating mischief.

King Herod has jurisdiction over the whole event. He condemns the bad Perchten to death and orders them bound with chains. But immediately afterward he reverses his decision, letting the mischief-makers off with a small fine, and the Perchtenlauf ends in a spirit of good will.

Another procession known as the *Glöcklerlauf* takes place in Styria. The Glöcklerlauf, or Bellringers Parade, is held annually on Epiphany Eve (January 5) in Ebensee on Traun Lake. Records show that the custom goes back at least 300 years; oral histories indicate that the parade may be even older.

Men and boys dress in white clothes, which fit in well with the snowy landscape. Around their hips and across their backs they hang a variety of noisemakers, including large, heavy bells. But the most impressive feature of the Glöcklerlauf costume is the huge, elaborate headdress worn by each of the bellcarriers. These amazing headdresses take months of work to create. A wooden frame in the shape of a star, pyramid, heart, or flower is covered with brightly colored silk or translucent paper and decorated with fanciful designs. These enormous "caps" weigh up to 15 kilograms (33 pounds) and sometimes exceed 3 meters (about 10 feet) in length.

When it is time for the Glöcklerlauf to begin, street lights, house lights, and store lights are extinguished throughout the Traun Lake area. The only light comes from the headdresses, which are illuminated from within by candles or electric flashlights. The participants look like immense Chinese lanterns with legs. All night long the bellcarriers race through the darkened streets of the Traun Lake market, admired by visitors from near and far.

The Glöcklerlauf seems to have derived from an ancient pagan spring ritual. The lights are symbolic of the lengthening days of spring, and the bells and other noisemakers are designed to chase away the winter.

Some Austrian families keep their Christmas trees until the feast of Candlemas in early February. But in most homes the tree is lit for the last time on January 6, the feast of the Epiphany, which brings the Twelve Nights to a close.

The Epiphany celebrates the arrival in Bethlehem of the *Drei Heiligen Könige*—the Three Holy Kings. One lovely, widespread Epiphany custom is *Sternsingen*, or "star singing." Youngsters dress up as the Three Kings (or Wise Men from the

Children dressed as the Three Kings move through the Austrian countryside on Epiphany. They carry make-believe gold, frankincense, and myrrh and receive hot chocolate and Lebkuchen *at their journey's end.*

East), often with faces painted white, red, and black to represent different human races. The star singers go from house to house, led by children bearing torches and lanterns. They are followed by a "star carrier," clad in a flowing white garment and carrying a shining star mounted on a long pole.

The Three Kings stand majestically before each house, singing of their journey over desert sands and mountains on their way to bring their precious gifts to the newborn Christ child. The head of the household often invites the group, in song, to pause and refresh themselves before continuing on their way. It is a rare star singer who fails to be tempted by hot chocolate and Lebkuchen

after such a long and difficult journey. Once refreshed, the Three Kings straighten their crowns, smooth out their robes, and proceed to the next house with renewed enthusiasm.

With the passing of the Epiphany, the Advent and Christmas seasons have run full cycle. With its combination of Christian beliefs and secular legends, the period of the Twelve Nights retains a charm and magic that the frantic pace of the twentieth century has not managed to erode.

Alpine Holidays

Sleigh bells jingle gaily with each hoofbeat as patient horses pull winter holiday-makers along an Alpine trail.

The majestic Alps and their foothills stretch across the western, southern, and central parts of Austria, a country justly famous for some of the most beautiful scenery in the world. It would be difficult to exaggerate the magnetic attraction that the mountains exercise over the Austrian character, or the pleasure they afford both those who live on their forested slopes and the many who take time out to experience the joys of the Christmas season that are unique to an Alpine holiday.

All over Austria, schools and offices officially close from Christmas Eve through St. Stephen's Day. Some city families take advantage of the time off and leave for a mountain holiday as soon as the Christmas Eve festivities are finished. For many Austrians, Christmas would not be Christmas without a ride in a horse-drawn sleigh through the sparkling snow and pure, clear air of one of Austria's postcard-pretty mountain retreats.

Many special events occur in the mountains and villages during the winter holiday season. Resort guests at Seefeld, high in the mountains in the Tirol region, mark the beginning of January with a skiing competition. In the village of Semmering in Lower Austria, near the mountain pass of the same name, the old year ends and the new one begins with a nighttime torchlight ski race. Ski instructors at Zürs (Vorarlberg) also begin the new year with a torchlight competition. In Dornbirn, the feast of the Epiphany is celebrated each year with a toboggan race.

The town of Landeck in the Upper Inn Valley is the site of an ancient and awe-inspiring rite. At dawn the young men of the area gather for a climb to the top of the craggy mountains that

The wintry whiteness and serenity of the Austrian Alps lure visitors to come enjoy a winter holiday.

Leaving an ocean of cars behind them, a determined family heads for the mountaintops. In Austria, where mountains cover three-fourths of the land, skiing is a sport that appeals to all ages.

surround the old city. There they build huge bonfires, which can be seen at dusk for many miles around. They also set fire to enormous pinewood disks that have been coated with tar, then set the fire wheels rolling down the mountainside to the valley below. The more courageous of the youths ski alongside the blazing wheels at harrowing speeds, carrying torches and shouting for all they are worth. The idea is to beat the wheels to the bottom of the mountain. People who witness this fiery annual event do not soon forget it.

Austria has an amazing variety of local customs and festivals, developed in the seclusion of Alpine valleys, yet enriched by contact with people of other regions. Many of them, such as the Glöcklerlauf and Perchtenlauf held during the Twelve Nights after Christmas, go back to a time when Christianity had not yet penetrated into Central Europe.

In ancient times, villagers set food aside for the Four Elements—earth, air, fire, and water. The custom survives as the Twelve Nights begin in certain parts of rural Austria, where farmers set down morsels of Christmas food at the roots of their fruit trees. The food is offered in hopes that the trees will bear fruit again during the coming year. Sleighloads of fodder are brought into the forests for the deer, so that even the wild animals can share the joys of Christmas.

Another Alpine practice on the first of the Twelve Nights is to collect *Christwurz* (*Helleborus niger*), a plant that once was thought highly effective against the plague and other maladies. Church bells ring and guns are fired to chase off any demons that might be on the loose as the mysterious Twelve Nights begin.

The custom of lighting Christmas trees on graves is spreading in rural Austria. This may be a holdover from earlier times, when lights were lit on All Souls' Day to warm the shivering ghosts that were said to hover around the graves.

The people of Tirol, Salzburg, and Carinthia practice a pagan counterpart to the Christian cus-

Huge-horned straw figures called Schab *rustle through the streets of the peaceful town of Mittendorf to clear the way for the St. Nicholas Eve parade.*

tom of Frauentragen. *Klöckler* or *Berchtl* nights are usually held the last three Thursdays before Christmas. The ritual takes various forms. In the Sarntal, boys in strange costumes run around making a racket with zithers, violins, cowbells, dish covers, and any other noisy instruments that come to hand. Two straw-covered figures called *Zuseln* occupy the center of the group, representing a husband and wife. The group moves from house to house. At each stop, the straw figures act out a comic domestic brawl, after which the whole bunch joins in a *Klöckellied*. This ancient song, in old German, tells the story of the Incarnation and includes a request for alms from the lady of the house. The singers have to answer some riddles before their request is granted.

In many villages, mystery pageants or folk dramas present a variety of religious and secular themes. The actors speak in regional dialects and wear traditional Alpine costumes.

Straw-clad characters also figure prominently in the annual *Nikolospiel* performed in the town of Mitterndorf. This combination parade and folk drama on December 5 depicts the arrival of Bishop Nicholas, the patron saint of children. The crack of whips and clang of bells announce the beginning of the parade. Straw figures known as *Schab,* with huge horns on their heads, lead the procession into town and clear the streets for the parade. They are followed by an assortment of other characters, including a policeman, a night watchman, and a feather-topped rider on a white horse. A man with a mask that bears smiling faces on all four sides carries a basket of sweets for the children.

The star of the show, St. Nicholas, is also preceded by sextons with collection bags, an angel,

A procession of Alpine villagers, carrying torches to light their way, moves toward the church for Christmas Eve midnight mass.

Delighted youngsters jockey for position atop the sled in this Alpine version of a Christmastime hayride.

In rural areas, Nativity plays bring to life the story of the birth of the Christ child.

and a "thunder bearer" carrying a large rod. St. Nicholas is accompanied by a local priest and followed by a beggar and the scythe-wielding character of Death. Lucifer, with a three-pronged fork, is chained by two other devils and hounded by a Marriage-Devil and several pairs of Krampuses in artful masks. The Nicholas-hunter brings up the rear of the procession, keeping order among the Krampuses.

As the parade approaches, a large crowd of children gathers in the main room of one of the local guesthouses or inns. The rider on the white horse rides around in circles in front of the inn, attempting to drive away evil spirits. Inside the inn, it is very quiet, until the thunder bearer jumps into the room and frightens the children. The angel quickly expels him, and St. Nicholas and the priest enter with a prayer: "Praise be to Jesus Christ."

The good bishop gives a sermon, and the priest quizzes the children to see if they know their prayers. When they have recited their lessons to Nicholas' satisfaction, the man with the smiling mask distributes sweets among the children.

The beggar begins a dialogue, but he is cut off in the middle by the figure of Death, swinging his scythe. Two Krampuses materialize at once to remove the body, and St. Nicholas admonishes everyone in the room to take to heart what just happened.

When the bishop and the priest leave the inn, the room is free for the powers of darkness. The Marriage-Devil, Lucifer, and various other evil characters prance about wildly, creating a terrible furor. Finally the sound of the night watchman's horn signals the end of the play. The reign of the evil ones is at an end, and they storm outside to join the other participants in the Nikolospiel as the parade moves on to the next guesthouse.

A considerably calmer rural Christmas custom is the tradition of "showing the Christ child." A sacristan and two altar boys carry a manger scene, or *Weihnachtskrippe*, from house to house, singing Christmas carols as they go. They are followed by a group of children dressed as shepherds and angels. At each house, the children are invited inside to perform little Nativity plays. The householders reward the youngsters with hot chocolate, Christmas cookies, and other treats before sending them on to their next stop.

In one charming variation of this Christmas tradition, the family living farthest from the village church starts down from the mountain carrying the manger and caroling by torchlight. When they reach the first house on their route, the neighbor family comes out to join them. Family after family joins the procession until at last it reaches the steps of the church. There a Nativity carol is sung and acted out: "Through the Darkness Gleams the Light." The entire village joins in on the final chorus, which announces the birth of the Christ child.

The beauty and richness of these Alpine customs are carried forth year after year by a people proud of their land and their traditions. Their spirit and friendliness warm the snowy winter landscape, bringing a sense of joy and peace to the holiday season in the Austrian mountains.

"Silent Night" and Strauss

Costumed carolers gather to sing "Silent Night, Holy Night," the most beloved of Austrian Christmas carols.

Austria's heritage of Christmas music—in particular its lovely, melodic folk carols—is rare in its charm and beauty. The *Hirtenlieder*, or shepherd songs, have delighted Austrians for centuries. In these rustic tunes, sung in the broadest dialect, the singers imagine themselves in the company of the shepherds of Bethlehem, addressing the newborn Christ child and his parents in simple, affectionate words. Many of these songs contain refrains that imitate the sounds of shepherds' instruments. Here is an especially playful stanza from an old Tirolean carol, "Jetzt hat sich halt aufgetan das himmlische Tor" ("The Gates of Heaven's Glory Did Spring Open Suddenly").

> So came we running to the crib,
>   I and also you,
> A bee-line into Bethlehem,
>   Hopsa, trala loo:
> "O baby dear, take anything
>   Of all the little gifts we bring:
> Have apples or have butter,
>   Maybe pears or yellow cheese;
> Or would you rather have some nuts,
>   Or plums, or what you please."
> Alleluja, alleluja;
>   Alle-, Alle-, Alleluja.

Because Austria's musical tradition is unusually rich and varied, Christmas carols for every mood echo from mountain villages and valley towns all through the holidays. Besides the shepherds' carols, there are lullaby carols, dance carols, companion carols, star carols, and those that can be performed properly only by yodelers.

The Silent Night Chapel in Oberndorf near Salzburg marks the spot where Franz Gruber and Joseph Mohr performed their song for the first time in 1818.

Though the original music for "Silent Night, Holy Night" vanished long ago, this is one of the oldest scores still in existence.

In the early 1800's especially, almost every local parish had its own poet, who delighted in adding new songs to the Christmas treasury. From this tradition sprang the most famous of Austria's contributions to the celebration of Christmas—the beloved "Stille Nacht, Heilige Nacht" ("Silent Night, Holy Night").

The story of the creation of this beautiful carol has been told time and time again in nations all over the world. Though some of the details have been altered in legend, the main outline of the story remains the same.

The words to the carol were written by the vicar of Oberndorf's St. Nicholas Church, Father Joseph Mohr, on Christmas Eve, 1818. One version has it that the local priest was inspired as he returned home in the wee hours of Christmas

Eve morning after blessing a newborn baby. The Napoleonic Wars were over, and peace reigned in Europe at last, especially in the settlement of Oberndorf, a village of sailors and farmers on the Salzach River. The majestic silence and beauty of the winter night prompted Father Mohr to hurry home and set down his immortal lines.

The parishioners of St. Nicholas had a problem on their hands that winter—the church organ was out of order. One version of the story maintains that mice had nibbled through the organ bellows. More likely, the instrument had been damaged by floodwaters. But in any event, Father Mohr wanted something special to make up for the lack of organ music at the Christmas Eve midnight mass.

The priest took the new Christmas poem to his friend Franz Gruber, a schoolteacher and church organist in the nearby village of Arnsdorf. Within a few hours, Gruber had composed the lyrical melody, so characteristic of Austrian folk music, that now is known throughout the world.

Both Gruber and Mohr were accomplished guitarists. In fact, they often entertained guests at local inns to supplement their meager salaries. Gruber brought his music to Father Mohr, and the two conducted a brief rehearsal with the St. Nicholas choir. "Silent Night, Holy Night" was performed for the first time at that evening's midnight mass, with much success. Mohr, a tenor, sang the melody; Gruber, a bass, sang harmony. The choir repeated the last two lines of each stanza in four-part harmony, and Mohr accompanied the voices on guitar.

The villagers were still talking about the simple, haunting strains of "Stille Nacht, Heilige Nacht" the following spring, when Carl Mauracher, an organ builder from the hamlet of Kapfing, near Fügen, Tirol, finally showed up to repair St. Nicholas' organ. The organ builder asked to hear the carol or to see a copy of the music. The authors evidently complied, perhaps even supplying Mauracher with the original score. We will never know, since the original music has long since been lost.

Mauracher, who had been asked to make the organ repairs before Christmas, was at least partly responsible for the song's creation. Had the organ been repaired, the song might never have been written. And Mauracher certainly played a major role in the carol's popularization. Mauracher took the tune back to his native Ziller Valley—a happy piece of luck, since the area was home to many traveling singers. From the Ziller Valley, the carol began its long and beautiful voyage around the world.

The first recorded performance of "Silent Night" outside Oberndorf was by a singing family called the Rainers in the village church of Fügen on Christmas Eve, 1819. Three years later, Austria's Emperor Francis I spent a couple of days in a castle near the village with Russia's Czar Alexander I. The Rainer family performed for the royal visitors. Among the tunes they sang was "Silent Night." The singers and their carol so enchanted the monarchs that the Rainers were invited to travel to Russia. Between 1824 and 1838 the family toured extensively.

Certain members of the family were responsible for introducing the carol to the United States. A group called the Rainer Quartet sang "Silent Night" before the Alexander Hamilton monument in New York City on Christmas Eve, 1839.

Joseph A. Rainer, a descendant of the original Rainer family, devoted a great deal of energy to preserving and popularizing the original melody.

Turmblasen, *chorale music played with brass instruments, punctuates Christmas Eve and New Year's Eve in many parts of Austria.*

In fact, he persuaded Dr. Albert Schweitzer to train his staff and patients at the Congo Hospital to sing the Christmas song.

Yet another singing group from the Ziller Valley helped to spread the lyrical melody of "Silent Night." Upon his return from Oberndorf, Mauracher taught the song to Caroline, Joseph, Andreas, and Amalie Strasser. Each year the Strasser children traveled to Leipzig in the kingdom of Saxony, the site of a giant annual trade fair. Their parents were glovemakers, and the children's job was to attract customers to their parents' display by singing Tirolean folk tunes.

The Strasser children were overheard by the director general of music in the kingdom of Saxony, who gave them tickets to one of the concerts that he regularly conducted in the guildhouse of the drapers of Leipzig. It happened that the concert

Vienna's holidays are brightened by the voices of the Vienna State Opera performing Die Fledermaus *at New Year's (top) and the Vienna Boys' Choir singing in Christmas services at the Hofburg (bottom).*

at the castle on Christmas Eve. And so it happened that on December 24, 1832, the Strasser children sang "Silent Night" at the Royal Saxon Court Chapel in Pleissenburg Castle.

By 1838 the song appeared in the *Leipziger Gesangbuch*, and in 1840 in a *Catholic Hymn and Prayer Book*. Less than a decade later, in 1849, a modified version of the song appeared in *Devotional Harmony*, an American Methodist compilation.

The king of Prussia, Frederick William IV, heard the carol for the first time in 1854, when it was sung by the entire choir of the Imperial Church in Berlin. It was not until that year that the royal chapel in Berlin began to make inquiries as to who had actually written and composed the carol.

By the 1840's "Silent Night" was being attributed to Haydn and Mozart, among others. Joseph Haydn's brother, Michael, had once or twice been a paying guest in the schoolhouse home of Franz Gruber, and many held that Michael Haydn must have composed the hymn.

On December 30, 1854, Franz Gruber wrote a letter to Berlin that set the record straight. By that time Gruber was 67 years old and served as an organist at the city church of Hallein. His letter contained proof that he had composed the music for the words provided by Father Mohr. Mohr had died in poverty in Wagrein, Salzburg, on December 4, 1848.

The old church of St. Nicholas no longer stands. But early in this century the town of Oberndorf commissioned a memorial to Mohr and Gruber. This memorial, the Silent Night Chapel, stands outside the new St. Nicholas Church. There were numerous available portraits of the teacher-composer, but not one likeness of the obscure priest who wrote the words. Father Mohr's body was exhumed from its pauper's grave in Wagrein, and its skull was sent to a sculptor in Vienna who attempted to create a likeness of Mohr based on the shape of his skull. The sculptor mistakenly returned the skull to Oberndorf instead of to Wagrein. To this day Father Joseph Mohr's skull rests beneath the Nativity scene in Oberndorf's Silent Night Chapel.

"Silent Night, Holy Night" is now sung by people of all nations. It is truly a song that went around the world and will stay with us for many generations to come. The small chapel that commemorates the carol's author and composer attracts tens of thousands of pilgrims every year. Shaped like an octagon, the chapel features a beautifully carved altar and stained-glass windows dedicated to Mohr and Gruber.

Though "Silent Night" has been translated into

was also attended by the king and queen of Saxony. At the close of the performance, the director announced that in the audience were four children with the finest voices he had heard in years. Could the children be persuaded to treat Their Royal Majesties to some of their lovely folk melodies? Among the Strassers' repertoire was the "Song of Heaven"—the children's name for "Silent Night." The carol so delighted the royal couple that they invited the children to perform it

Vienna's monument to Johann Strauss, the "Waltz King," stands frozen in the snow.

every major language in the world, its simplicity and harmony are characteristic of the countryside around Salzburg. The compositions of the region's greatest son, Wolfgang Amadeus Mozart, also reflect the musical heritage of the Austrian countryside, and their appeal is universal.

Austria has produced an extraordinary number of the world's great composers. Besides Mozart, the list includes Joseph Haydn and Franz Schubert, whose "Ave Maria," one of the loveliest songs ever written, delights Christmas audiences to this day.

Both Haydn and Schubert were members of the Vienna Boys' Choir, whose continued existence over a period of more than 500 years is another testament to the Austrian musical genius. Christmas in Vienna would not be Christmas without this magnificent choir.

New Year's, on the other hand, would simply not be New Year's without the delightful melodies of Johann Strauss, the "Waltz King." The Vienna Philharmonic Orchestra helps celebrate the New Year with its annual all-Strauss concert of waltzes and polkas. Another beloved tradition is the annual New Year's Eve performance of the Strauss operetta *Die Fledermaus* by the Vienna State Opera. And as Austrians whirl through the Fasching season, they do so to the tune of Strauss waltzes.

Visions of
Vienna

At Christmas, the streets of Vienna are transformed into a fairy-tale land of color and light.

Vienna at Christmastime is a symphony for the senses. Sights, sounds, smells, tastes, and textures combine in a happy whirl of excitement. Days are short; on Christmas Eve the sun doesn't rise until nearly eight o'clock, and it sets just after four. The sun's warmth is often blocked by a heavy layer of clouds, and the mercury usually stands below freezing. Still, during the holidays, the capital is cheerful. Vienna lights up like a Christmas tree. Thousands of colored lights, arranged in every conceivable Christmas motif, twinkle and glitter along the main streets. Most Vienna Christmases are white. Set like a jewel in the snowy landscape, the city looks exceptionally romantic.

On Christmas Eve, icicles hang from Vienna's roofs and windowsills. Paper vendors, clad in high boots and long woolen scarves, slap their hands across their chests to keep warm. They exhale little puffs of steam, like old-fashioned locomotives. Every few blocks, the warm red glow of a chestnut vendor's stove attracts a ring of last-minute shoppers. Paper cones of hot roasted chestnuts will tide them over until Christmas Eve dinner.

By early evening, around six or so, most shops and restaurants have closed their doors, and the Viennese are home preparing for the evening's festivities. After dinner and the exchange of gifts, the whole city eagerly awaits the midnight bells that call the faithful to worship. It is hard to imagine Christmas Eve in Vienna without the deep, ringing booms and melodious tones that joyfully announce the birth of Christkindl.

Vienna is a musical city at any time of the year. But Christmas has its own special sounds, from

Snow-crowned Vienna is one of the world's most charming cities at Christmastime.

the delightful street organs that captivate the city's children to the Turmblasen, the Christmas music that trumpets forth from St. Stephen's Cathedral and the steeple of the Guildhall every Christmas Eve.

The angelic voices of the Vienna Boys' Choir traditionally ring out on Christmas Eve in the Burgkappel at the Hofburg, formerly the private chapel of the Hapsburg Castle in downtown Vienna. The choir also sings on Christmas Day and at services on St. Stephen's Day, December 26. Instrumentalists, as well as tenors and basses from the Vienna State Opera, supplement the boys' sopranos and altos. Nothing much has changed in the choir's performance since the chapel was built in the late 1400's—except, of course, that the youngsters have become famous all over the world.

One of the most sensuous experiences to be had in Vienna at Christmastime is a visit to one of its many pastry shops. Demel's pastry shop, the world's top-ranking *Konditorei* (confectioner), offers a magnificent annual Christmas display. Gorgeous fairy-tale landscapes feature chocolate Tirolean chalets, butter-creamy meadows, marzipan glaciers, and luscious stylized Christmas trees. Even Viennese who can't afford the calories or expense of a *Schaumrolle* (puff-pastry filled with whipped cream) or *Doboschtorte* (rich, chocolate-filled cake with caramel topping) can feast their eyes for free.

It is said that Demel's represents the Viennese *Lebensart,* the city's manner of living, its sweet way of life. The shop is both a national monument and Austria's gastronomic conscience. Demel's uses nothing but the finest ingredients from all over the world. The shop even mixes its own chocolate from selected cocoa beans and sugar. It takes no less than 72 hours to produce a confection so delicious it might have been made in paradise by the Christmas angels themselves.

Demel's was founded in 1786 by Ludwig Dehne, a sugar baker's apprentice from Württemberg, who set up shop across from the stage door of the old Burg Theater. Dehne's beautifully

A hand-painted street organ pipes a merry tune while a whimsical toy monkey delights two youngsters in downtown Vienna.

Just a glance at this stunning selection in Demel's pastry shop demonstrates why Viennese pastries are famous around the world.

Christmas shoppers pause for rest and refreshment at one of Vienna's legendary coffee houses.

At the Hofburg's Spanish Riding School, founded in Vienna in 1580, the famous Lippizan horses perform a spellbinding series of cavalry exercises.

Linzertorte
(Linzer cake)

Pastry:
1½ cups all-purpose flour
¼ cup sugar
½ tsp. baking powder
½ tsp. salt
½ tsp. cinnamon
½ cup brown sugar, firmly packed
½ cup unsalted butter (no substitutions)
1 egg, slightly beaten
½ cup finely ground unblanched almonds
blanched slivered almonds for decoration

Filling:
2 cups raspberry jam

1. Mix flour, sugar, baking powder, salt, and cinnamon. Using a pastry blender or two knives, cut in brown sugar and butter until mixture resembles coarse meal.
2. Add the egg and ground almonds, and blend with a fork until mixture forms a ball. Wrap half the pastry and chill.
3. Press remaining half of pastry into the bottom and up the sides of an 8-inch spring-form pan. Bake at 350° for 20 minutes.

To assemble:
4. Roll remaining dough into an 8-inch circle and cut strips ½ inch wide.
5. Spread jam in partially baked shell.
6. Arrange dough strips in a lattice pattern over filling. (Use 1 or 2 of the long strips to cover lattice ends around rim.) Press gently to seal. Press some blanched slivered almonds into dough.
7. Bake at 350° for 30 minutes until lightly browned. May be eaten warm.

Yield: 1 8-inch torte

Wigged musicians in period costumes revive the elegance of the Austrian Empire at Vienna's annual Emperor's Ball on New Year's Eve.

crafted ice-cream creations, doughnuts, and cookies were a favorite with the leading ladies who performed at the theater across the street. Unfortunately, Dehne didn't live to see his wife become court caterer and his shop named the official sugar bakery of the imperial household. The business left the family in 1857, when Christoph Demel bought the shop from the founder's grandson. Thirty years later Demel moved his pastry shop to its current location in the Kohlmarkt, where it now enjoys landmark status.

You probably lack the patience to mix your own chocolate for 72 hours. But following the recipe for *Linzertorte* can bring the delights of Viennese pastry to your palate with relatively little effort.

The most important event in Vienna on New Year's Eve is the Emperor's Ball at the Hofburg. Some 1400 guests from every continent gather to celebrate the holiday in the tradition of the old Austrian monarchy. Everyone dresses formally—in white tie and tails or in elegant ball gowns—and the musicians' period costumes give the im-

pression that the event is taking place in another century.

Guests are greeted with cocktails shortly before eight, and ladies receive a memento from a woman dressed as the empress. Dinner is served in several halls while the costumed musicians play Strauss waltzes. After dinner the guests congregate in the main hall for the official New Year's celebration—a one-hour performance with professional dancers. The whole affair lasts until around five in the morning.

Vienna is the only world capital where balls are the main winter social activity. The events are as elegant and proper as in the days of the Empire. The Emperor's Ball marks the beginning of the season known as Fasching. Seven weeks and 300 balls later, Fasching comes to an end. But glorious visions of Vienna play on and on in our dreams.

Christmas Expressions

Hand-carved scenes depicting the birth of Christ have been an Austrian tradition for hundreds of years.

Austrian villagers, cattle farmers, and shepherds—the inhabitants of the country's secluded Alpine valleys—have long been forced to create their own entertainments, diversions, and cultural expressions. Their mountain isolation has encouraged a great variety of folk arts, from woodworking to folk songs and poetry.

No theme has drawn a more enthusiastic response from Austria's talented folk artists than the joy and wonder of Christmas, perhaps best expressed in the magnificent *Weihnachtskrippen* (Nativity scenes) that occupy a prominent place in almost every Austrian church and home during the Christmas holidays.

The *Krippe* seems to have originated in medieval Christmas plays and the Late Gothic Christmas altars occasioned by these plays. The Christmas plays gave rise to the *Landschaftskrippe*, the most frequently seen type of Krippe in Austria. In the Landschaftskrippe, the Nativity scene is set before the city of Bethlehem. Sometimes the Holy Family is sheltered in a cave, or occasionally amid the ruins of King David's castle, indicating Jesus' ancestry. Bethlehem may be depicted as a fanciful oriental settlement. But most often the Holy Family is shown in a typical Austrian stable, and Bethlehem looks like an Austrian village.

The movable figures of the Landschaftskrippe always include the Holy Family, of course, and usually a selection of shepherds, angels, and animals. The main figures are often dressed in the costumes of the Austrian region in which they were created. Minor characters may be clothed in more varied fashions.

Some of the more elaborate Krippen feature

Some churches display very large and elaborate Nativity scenes, many with a distinct Alpine character.

*Wood is a favorite medium for handmade Krippen,
but other materials are also employed, including wax,
porcelain, and earthenware.*

dozens and dozens of figures, often engaged in activities having nothing to do with the Nativity itself. Hunters may chase deer through the mountains above Bethlehem. In the town itself we might see a cobbler working away with awl and twine and a blacksmith striking a hot iron. Soldiers costumed in eighteenth-century uniforms snap to attention on King Herod's orders.

The *Kastenkrippe,* a form predominant in the Salzkammergut, derives from Late Gothic Christmas altars. Fixed figures appear in a landscape rising steeply to the background; the Krippe is boxlike, with a glass window in front.

Old genuine Krippen are highly prized. A number of Nativities have found their way into museums, including Vienna's Folklore Museum and the Christmas Crib Museum in Saalfelden's Ritzen Castle.

Carved shepherds and angels, handwrought dolls and hobby horses, paintings and delicate woodcuts, elaborate pastries, and intricate ornaments—all these symbols of Christmas are lovingly created by Austrian artists and artisans. Their beauty enhances the music, the dancing, the traditions, the faith, and the family warmth that is Christmas in Austria.

The Bauer Company in Vienna has been making hand-carved rocking horses since the 1800's. The present owner, shown at work in his studio, is the founder's grandson.

A classic cavalry pose of the famous Lippizan horses has been reproduced in gingerbread, down to the smallest detail.

Lovely folk paintings are displayed next to a collection of handcrafted dolls, lovingly fashioned from colorful material and yarn.

Austrian Treats

Aprikosenblättergebäck
(apricot leaves)

In this delightful woodcut, based on an 1848 drawing by Fritz Bergen, a generous Hausfrau rewards some young New Year's singers (above).

A display of luscious treats (left) is topped by Ischler Törtchen and Pfeffernüsse. Spicy Lebkuchen appear next to a Stollen surrounded by Aprikosenblättergebäck. Spanish Wind cookies complete the picture.

½ cup butter
⅓ cup sugar
1 egg
½ tsp. vanilla
¼ tsp. grated lemon rind
1 cup flour
¼ tsp. salt

1. Blend butter and sugar until creamy. Beat in egg and vanilla.
2. Mix remaining ingredients together. Add to butter mixture and mix well. Chill dough several hours.
3. Preheat oven to 375°. Pinch off pieces of dough and form into 1½-inch balls. Roll balls in sugar and place 2 inches apart on lightly greased and floured cookie sheet. Bake 5 minutes.
4. Carefully make an indentation in the center of each cookie with the backside of a round ¼ teaspoon or with the handle end of a wooden spoon. Return to oven and bake 8 additional minutes, until edges are slightly brown. While warm, fill centers with apricot jam. Cool on rack.

Yield: about 2–3 dozen cookies

Striezel
(twist bread)

1 package dry yeast
¼ cup warm water (105°–115°)
pinch of sugar
½ cup milk, heated and cooled
¼ cup sugar
½ tsp. salt
¼ tsp. grated lemon rind
2 Tbsp. butter, soft
1 egg
2½ to 3 cups flour
½ cup raisins

1. Sprinkle yeast over ¼ cup warm water. Add pinch of sugar and stir to dissolve. Let stand 3–5 minutes.

2. Combine milk, sugar, salt, lemon rind, and butter in large bowl. Add egg, 1½ cups flour, and yeast mixture. Beat until smooth— about 100 strokes. Blend in raisins. Stir in rest of flour, ½ cup at a time, to form soft dough.

3. Turn dough onto a lightly floured board. Knead by hand about 8 minutes, until dough is smooth and elastic. Place in greased bowl and lightly grease top and sides of dough with fingers. Cover with plastic wrap and let rise in warm spot (80°–85°) until dough has doubled in bulk, about 1½ hours.

4. Punch down dough and place on lightly floured board. With sharp knife, divide dough into 4 equal parts. Let dough rest 10 minutes.

5. Shape 3 of the 4 pieces into smooth rolled ropes about 14 inches long. Place side by side on greased baking sheet (11 inches by 17 inches). Weave the 3 ropes into a tight braid. Pinch ends together and tuck under.

6. Divide fourth piece of dough into 3 equal pieces. Shape into rolled ropes about 10 inches long. Make a second braid and place on top of first braid, using wooden toothpicks to hold in place if necessary.

7. Cover with wax paper and let rise in warm place until double in bulk, about 1 hour.

8. Preheat oven to 400°. Bake for 10 minutes at 400°. Turn temperature down to 350° and bake 35–40 minutes longer. Bread is done if it sounds hollow when tapped on bottom crust.

9. If desired, immediately after removing bread from oven, brush with a small amount of melted butter to soften crust.

Yield: 1 loaf

Honigbusserl
(honey kisses)

⅓ cup melted unsalted butter
1 cup honey
2 eggs
½ cup milk
3½ cups all-purpose flour
2 tsp. baking powder
½ tsp. baking soda
1 tsp. cinnamon
½ tsp. allspice
1 cup raisins

1. Combine melted butter and honey. Add eggs and milk and blend.

2. Mix flour and spices and add to butter mixture. Stir in raisins.

3. Drop walnut-sized pieces of dough onto a lightly greased cookie sheet.

4. Bake at 375° for 12–15 minutes.

Yield: about 4–5 dozen cookies

Ischler Törtchen
(raspberry tartlets)

½ lb. plus 4 Tbsp. unsalted butter
  (2½ sticks)
⅔ cup sugar
2 cups all-purpose flour
1¾ cups ground almonds
⅛ tsp. cinnamon
½ cup raspberry jam
confectioners' sugar

1. Cream the butter and sugar until light and fluffy. Add flour, ½ cup at a time, along with the cinnamon and almonds. Beat until mixture becomes a slightly stiff dough.
2. Shape the dough into a ball and wrap in plastic wrap. Refrigerate for ½ hour.
3. Divide the dough in half. On a lightly floured surface, roll half the dough out to ⅛-inch thickness.
4. Using a 2½-inch to 3-inch cookie cutter, cut as many circles from the dough as you can. Collect the scraps and roll the dough again, cutting more circles. You should have about 12. Place circles on an ungreased cookie sheet.
5. Roll out the remaining half of the dough, and cut out circles in the same manner. But before arranging this second group of circles on a cookie sheet, cut out the center of each circle with a ½-inch cookie cutter.
6. Bake both groups of circles at 325° for 10–13 minutes or until lightly browned. With a metal spatula, gently ease the cookies onto a wire rack and allow to cool.

To assemble:

7. Spread raspberry jam on each solid circle.
8. Dust the cut-out cookies with confectioners' sugar. Then place one cut-out cookie on top of each jam-coated solid cookie. Press gently.

Yield: 12 tartlets

Topfenknödel
(cheese dumplings)

15 oz. farmer cheese
4 eggs
¼ tsp. salt
¾ cup matzo meal
3 Tbsp. butter
½ cup fine bread crumbs

1. Mash the farmer cheese in a bowl using a potato masher. Still using the masher, add the eggs and salt. Gradually add the matzo meal. The dough will be quite firm. Chill for 2 hours.
2. Bring 3 quarts water to the simmering point. Form the mixture into dumplings 1½ inches in diameter. Lower the dumplings into the simmering water and cook, uncovered, for 30 minutes or until dumplings rise to the surface and roll themselves over. (Do not stir.)
3. Remove dumplings one at a time using a slotted spoon and drain in a colander.
4. Melt the butter in a small saucepan. Add the bread crumbs and cook for 2–3 minutes until crumbs are crisp and lightly browned. Add the dumplings, cover the pan, and shake the pan back and forth over the heat until the dumplings are hot and coated with the toasted bread crumbs.

Serve Topfenknödel hot with jam or stewed fruit.

Yield: about 14–16 dumplings

Austrian Accents

Christkindl
(Christ Child ornament)

1. & 2.

Assemble:

2-inch wooden doll form (from a crafts supplies store) *or* a round wooden clothespin

6-inch by 2-inch piece of gauze bandage

4¾-inch by 6-inch piece of cotton fabric with small print

25-inch piece of colored cotton cord to match fabric

fine-tip felt marking pen

pinking shears to cut fabric

1. Draw a face on the head of the doll form or clothespin with marking pen.

2. Wrap the wooden figure in the gauze. Starting with the head, cover all of the head and body except the face.

3. Lay the piece of fabric on a table, with the wrong side of the fabric facing up. Place the gauze-wrapped figure lengthwise at the center of one 4¾-inch end of the fabric. The figure should be lying facedown, with the head hanging over the end of the fabric. Fold both sides of the cloth around the figure so it is in a tube of cloth from the neck down.

4. Fold the bottom of the tube of fabric up behind the figure's head.

5. Wrap the cord around figure and cloth to secure the figure in the cloth. Knot the cord in back of the neck. Make a second knot at the ends of the cord to form a loop.

This ornament may be hung on the Christmas tree or placed in a cradle in a manger scene.

3.

4.

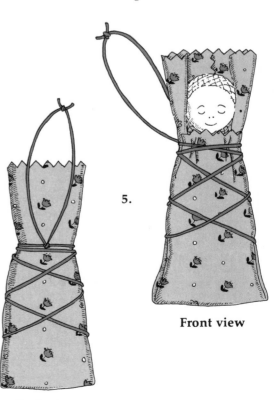

5.

Front view

Back view

Glücksbringer Schwein aus Marzipan
(*"Good luck" marzipan pigs*)

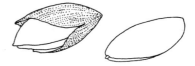

Ingredients:
1 cup finely ground blanched
  (skinless) almonds*
1 cup confectioners' sugar
1 egg white, unbeaten
a few drops of rosewater (or water
  if rosewater is not available)
red food coloring

Assemble:
bowl
pastry brush
wax paper
rolling pin
table knife

*It is important that almonds are blanched (skinless) and very finely ground. If ground blanched almonds are not available, you may grind whole blanched almonds. Or you may blanch and skin whole almonds yourself before grinding.

To blanch and skin whole almonds: Place approximately 1½ cups shelled almonds in a bowl. Pour boiling water over almonds. Let stand briefly in boiling water to loosen skins, but not for more than 1 minute. Pour almonds into colander to remove water. Pinch and pull loose skins off almonds. Let dry overnight before grinding.

To grind whole blanched almonds: Grind approximately 1½ cups whole blanched almonds very fine, using a blender, coffee grinder, or hand grinder.

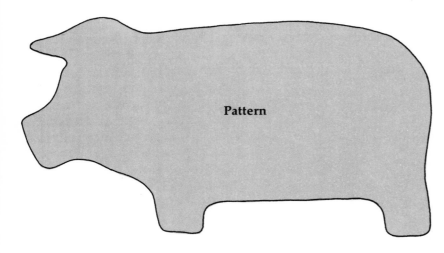

Pattern

1. To make marzipan dough, combine 1 cup ground blanched almonds and 1 cup confectioners' sugar in a bowl. Add the unbeaten white of 1 egg and a few drops of rosewater (or plain water). Sprinkle hands with confectioners' sugar to prevent sticking. Knead the mixture to make a smooth dough.

2. Roll out the dough between 2 sheets of wax paper to about ¼-inch thickness.

3. Using a table knife, draw the outline of a pig in the dough. (Or you may make a paper pattern from the drawing provided and use the pattern to cut out the pigs.) Pull away the excess dough and save to make other pigs.

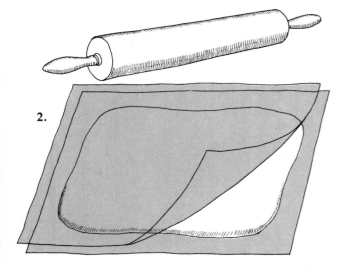

2.

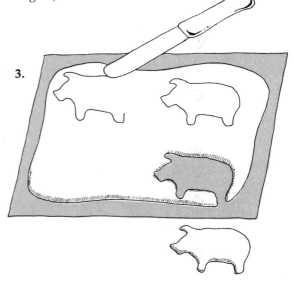

3.

4. Use small pieces of dough to shape ears, eyes, and tail. Lightly draw in mouth with knife.

5. Let pigs harden for 24 hours. Then use pastry brush to paint the pigs pink, using red food coloring diluted with water.

Yield: 6 pigs (approximately 4 inches by 2 inches)

These marzipan pigs may be eaten or used for decoration at New Year's celebrations. Or if you'd like to follow the Austrian tradition, give them to friends as *Glücksbringer*, to wish them good luck in the New Year.

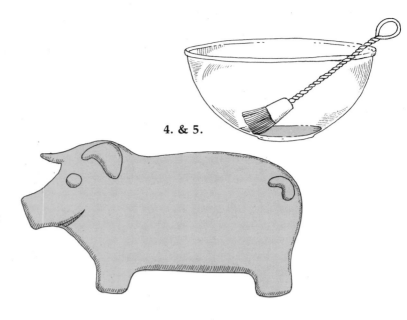

4. & 5.

Sun and moon ornaments

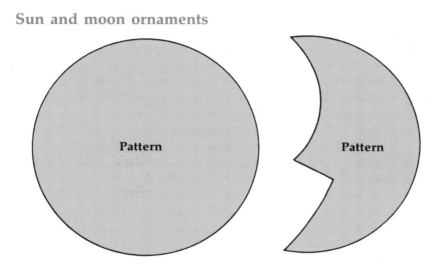

Pattern

Pattern

Assemble:
yellow poster board
¼-inch-wide flat braided or woven straw *or* flattened paper drinking straws *or* natural broom straw
jar lid (about 2¼ inches across)
scissors
pencil
white glue
cotton-tipped swabs
2 8-inch pieces of heavy gold cord
fine-tip felt marking pen

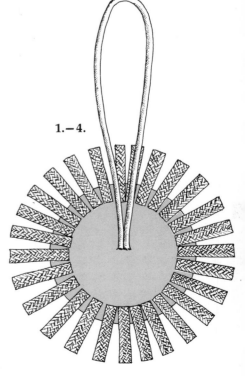

1.—4.

1. From the yellow poster board, cut out 2 circles for the sun and 2 crescents (about ⅗ circles) for the moon. Use the jar lid as a circle pattern. (Or make paper patterns for the sun and moon from the drawings provided.)

2. Cut straw in 1-inch pieces—about 26 pieces for the sun and 13 pieces for the moon.

3. Attach 1-inch pieces of straw braid (or straws) around the edge of each ornament as follows: Cover the inside of 1 sun circle with a light coat of glue, using fingers or cotton-tipped swabs. Also apply glue to about ¼ inch of the end of each piece of straw. Press each straw down firmly on the glued side of the sun circle so that ¼ inch of each straw is on the sun and the rest extends beyond the edge. Continue attaching straw pieces (about 26) until the outer edge is filled. Straw pieces should fan out like rays of light. Then attach straw pieces to one moon crescent in the same manner, applying glue to the inside of the crescent and attaching about 13 straw pieces to the outside edge.

4. Take an 8-inch piece of cord and cover about ½ inch of each end with glue. Press both ends of the cord together. Then press both ends onto the straw-filled inside of the sun circle. Position cord ends at the top of the ornament so the cord can be used as a loop for hanging. Attach the other 8-inch cord to the straw-filled inside of the moon crescent in the same manner. Make sure the cords and straws are firmly in place.

5. Cover the inside of the matching sun circle with glue. Align the 2 circles, inside to inside, and press firmly together. Glue the 2 moon crescents together in the same manner. Put ornaments under a heavy book or other weight for at least 15 minutes to dry.

6. If desired, use a fine-tip felt marking pen to draw faces on one or both sides of each ornament.

Hang the sun and moon ornaments on the Christmas tree to add a traditional Austrian touch.

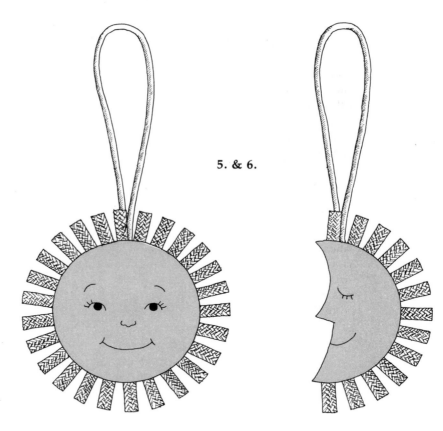

5. & 6.

Angel

Assemble:
6-inch wooden doll form (from a crafts supplies store) *or* a round wooden clothespin, large size
gold, silver, and blue foil paper*
gold stars with adhesive backs
18-gauge copper wire, 10½ inches long
2 natural-color pre-drilled wooden beads, about ⁷⁄₁₆-inch diameter
white glue

needle and quilting thread or other strong thread
fine-tip felt marking pen
scissors
ruler
pencil

*If colored heavy foil-sided paper is not available, foil gift-wrap or construction paper may be substituted.

First assemble each part of the angel, following the instructions in steps 1–6.

1. *Skirt:* Cut out a 6-inch by 12-inch piece of gold foil paper. Make a 6-inch-high skirt by pleating the foil in ½-inch folds. With the pleats folded together, use needle to run an 18-inch-long thread through pleats at top of skirt.

1.

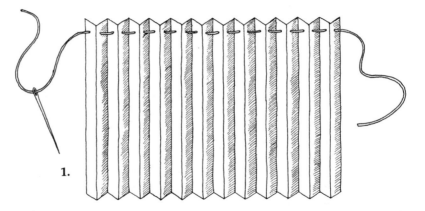

Patterns*

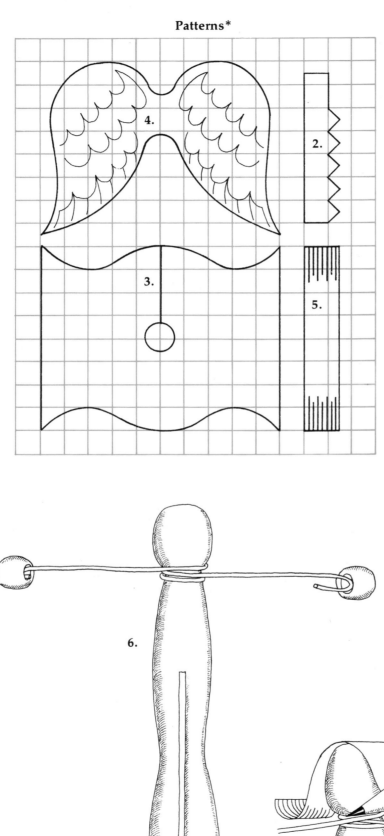

2. *Crown:* Cut a 3½-inch by ¾-inch piece of gold foil paper. Cut points (about ¼-inch deep and ½-inch wide) across 2½ inches of the crown. Then cut a ¼-inch-deep strip off the remaining 1 inch (on same side as points).

3. *Top of gown:* Cut a 5-inch by 4-inch piece of blue foil paper. Cut out a circle (⅝-inch in diameter) in the center. Then make a cut from that circle to the middle of one of the 5-inch-long sides. Cut curved edge along both 5-inch-long sides as shown. Cover the foil side with adhesive gold stars.

4. *Wings:* Cut two 5-inch by 3¾-inch pieces of silver foil paper. Glue the two pieces back-to-back to form a piece that is silver on both sides. Cut to shape a pair of wings (as shown). If desired, lightly draw in feathers with a pencil.

5. *Hair:* Cut a 4-inch by ¾-inch piece of silver foil paper. Make cuts about ¾-inch deep into each end to form fringes.

6. *Arms:* Place the doll form or clothespin in the center of the copper wire. Wind each end of the wire once around the doll form at the neck. Fold back each end of wire about ½ inch. Slip a wooden bead onto bent part of wire at each end so bead fits snugly.

Now put the parts of the angel together, following the instructions in steps 7–12.

7. Glue the hair onto the head of the doll form or clothespin. Roll fringed ends around a pencil so that hair curls up.

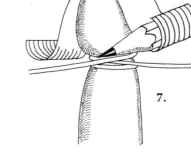

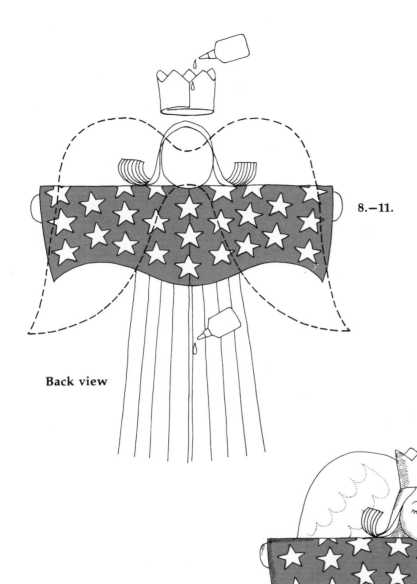

Back view

8.—11.

8. Put the skirt around the figure and tie the threads at the back of the neck. Glue together the last folds on each side of the skirt.

9. Place top of gown over arms and around neck of figure, slit side at the back. Use gold stars or glue to connect the two sides of back of gown top. Roll both sides of gown top down over arms, and attach front and back of gown top under the hands with a little glue.

10. Glue the crown on top of the head.

11. Glue the wings to the back of the gown top or to the back of the head, as desired.

12. Draw face in with marking pen.

The angel is ready to stand on a table or mantel or to put on top of a Christmas tree.

*Patterns shown are ½ actual size (shown on graph paper with ¼-inch squares). To double size of patterns, draw same shapes on paper with ½-inch squares.

12.

Front view

Austrian Melodies

Silent Night, Holy Night
(Stille Nacht, Heilige Nacht)

Joseph Mohr, 1818
Translation: Anonymous, from C.L. Hutchins'
Sunday School Hymnal, 1871

Franz Gruber, 1818

2. *Stille Nacht, heilige Nacht!*
   Hirten erst kundgemacht!
   Durch der Engel Halleluja
   Tönt es laut von fern und nah:
   Christ, der Retter, ist da,
   Christ, der Retter, ist da!

3. *Stille Nacht, heilige Nacht!*
   Gottes Sohn, O, wie lacht
   Lieb aus deinem göttlichen Mund,
   Da uns schlägt die rettende Stund,
   Christ, in deiner Geburt,
   Christ, in deiner Geburt.

2. Silent night, holy night,
   Shepherds quake at the sight;
   Glories stream from heaven afar,
   Heavenly hosts sing alleluia,
   Christ, the Savior, is born!
   Christ, the Savior, is born!

3. Silent night, holy night,
   Son of God, love's pure light
   Radiant beams from Thy holy face,
   With the dawn of redeeming grace,
   Jesus, Lord, at Thy birth,
   Jesus, Lord, at Thy birth.

The Twilight Is Falling

(Es Wird Scho Glei Dumpa)

Traditional Austrian

Traditional Austrian

Andante

1. Es — wird scho glei dum - pa, es wird jå schon Nåcht. Drum —
1. The twi - light is fall - ing, and on steals the night; I —

kimm i zu Dir — her, mein Hei - land auf d'Wåcht. Will
come to Thee, Je - sus, my Heav - en - ly Light. I

sin - gan a Lia - dl dem — Liab - ling dem Kloan. Du —
come to Thy cra - dle and — sing Thee a song; I —

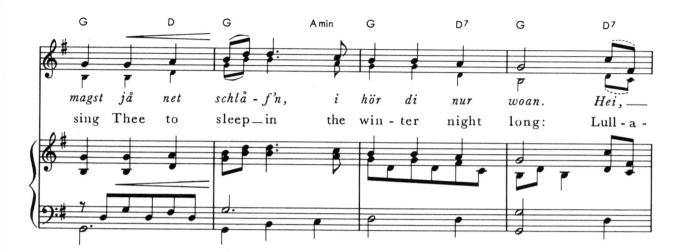

magst jå net schlå-f'n, i hör di nur woan. Hei,—
sing Thee to sleep—in the win-ter night long: Lull-a-

hei, hei,— hei, schlaf — süass, herz - liabs — Kind!
by, lull - a - by, Sweet-ly sleep, dear - est — Child!

2. *Schliass zua deine Augerl in Ruah und in Fried,*
Und gib ma zum Abschied dein Segn nur grad mit.
Aft wird ja mei Schlaferl a sorgenlos sein.
Aft kann i mi ruahli aufs Niederlegn freun.
Hei, hei, hei, hei, schlaf süass, herzliabs-Kind!

2. Oh, close Thy tired eyes, now, and drift into sleep.
Although I must leave Thee, Thy blessing I'll keep.
I go to my slumber and rest without care,
Because Thou art near me, my Savior so fair.
Lullaby, lullaby—sweetly sleep, dearest Child.

Still, Still, Still

Traditional Austrian

Salzburg melody, 1819

1. Still, __ still, __ still, Weil's __ Kind - lein __ schla - fen __ will! Ma -

1. Still, __ still, __ still, He __ sleeps this __ night so __ chill! The

ri - a __ tut es nie - der __ sin - gen, Ih - re __ keu - sche Brust dar - brin - gen,

Vir - gin's __ ten - der arms en - fold - ing, Warm and __ safe the Child are __ hold - ing,

Still,__ still,__ still,   Weil __ Kind - lein __ schla - fen __ will.
Still,__ still,__ still,   He __ sleeps this __ night so __ chill.

2. *Schlaf, schlaf, schlaf,*
   Mein liabes Kindlein, schlaf!
   Die Engel tuan schö musizieren,
   Bei dem Kindlein jubilieren,
   Schlaf, schlaf, schlaf,
   Mein liabes Kindlein, schlaf!

2. Sleep, sleep, sleep,
   He lies in slumber deep
   While angel hosts from heav'n come
      winging,
   Sweetest songs of joy are singing,
   Sleep, sleep, sleep,
   He lies in slumber deep.

Acknowledgments

Cover inset: Maxine Hesse, Fotomax
Cover: Bildarchiv Hans Huber KG
2:   © Vaccaro, Louis Mercier
6:   Maxine Hesse, Fotomax
7:   Salzburg City Tourist Office
8:   (Top) Michael Heiss
     (Bottom) Maxine Hesse, Fotomax
9:   Space
10:   Internationale Bilderagentur
11:   Maxine Hesse, Fotomax
12:   © Inge Morath, Magnum
13:   Internationale Bildarchiv
14:   © Lily Solmssen, Photo Researchers
15:   Maxine Hesse, Fotomax
16:   Bavaria-Verlag
17:   Post- und Telegraphendirektion
18:   © Vaccaro, Louis Mercier
19:   Michael Heiss
20:   Maxine Hesse, Fotomax
21:   Maxine Hesse, Fotomax
23:   (Top) Maxine Hesse, Fotomax
     (Bottom) Maxine Hesse, Fotomax
24:   Austrian Press and Information Service
25:   (Top) Maxine Hesse, Fotomax
     (Bottom) Michael Heiss
26:   (Top) Space
     (Bottom) Cosy-Verlag
29:   Space
30:   (Top) Space
     (Bottom) Space
31:   Cosy-Verlag
32:   © Vaccaro, Louis Mercier
33:   Fremdenverkehrsverband für Wien
34:   Stadtverkehrsbüro Salzburg
35:   (Top) Space
     (Bottom) © Lily Solmssen, Photo Researchers
37:   Austrian National Tourist Office
38:   (Top) Maxine Hesse, Fotomax
     (Bottom) © Vaccaro, Louis Mercier
39:   © Inge Morath, Magnum
40:   Internationale Bilderagentur
41:   © Vaccaro, Louis Mercier
42:   Cosy-Verlag
43:   Colour Library International
44:   © Milt and Joan Mann
45:   © Helmut Kain
46:   (Top) Austrian National Tourist Office
     (Bottom) © Vaccaro, Louis Mercier
47:   O. Hofer, Fremdenverkehrsverband Innsbruck-Igls und Umgebung
48:   Bavaria-Verlag
49:   Cosy-Verlag
50:   Bavaria-Verlag
51:   © Vaccaro, Louis Mercier
52:   (Top) Space
     (Bottom) Space
53:   Fremdenverkehrsverband für Wien
54:   Fremdenverkehrsverband für Wien
55:   Fremdenverkehrsverband für Wien
56:   © Buck
57:   (Top) Space
     (Bottom) Space
58:   Austrian National Tourist Office
59:   Space
60:   D. Defner, Fremdenverkehrsverband Innsbruck-Igls und Umgebung
61:   Pinzgauer Heimatmuseum
62:   Austrian Institute Library
63:   (Top) Space
     (Bottom) Space
     (Right) Space
64:   WORLD BOOK photo by Robert Frerck
65:   Bildarchiv Preussischer Kulturbesitz